FONDUE

THE FINE ART OF FONDUE, CHINESE WOK AND CHAFING DISH COOKING

PUBLISHER: R. ARTHUR BARRETT
EDITOR: CAROL D. BRENT
ART DIRECTOR: DICK COLLINS
PHOTOGRAPHY BY BILL MILLER

Book Trade Distribution by
DOUBLEDAY & COMPANY, INC.
Garden City, New York

TESTED RECIPE PUBLISHERS, INC. CHICAGO

CONTENTS-FONDUES

FIRST EDITION
FIRST PRINTING AUGUST 1969
SECOND PRINTING NOVEMBER 1969
THIRD PRINTING JANUARY 1970
FOURTH PRINTING APRIL 1970

REVISED EDITION
FIFTH PRINTING NOVEMBER 1970
SIXTH PRINTING MAY 1971
SEVENTH PRINTING AUGUST 1971
EIGHTH PRINTING JANUARY 1973

ISBN 0-88351-000-6
Library of Congress Catalog Card Number 77-95289

OTHER FINE GOURMET INTERNATIONAL™ BOOKS:

BARBECUE: The Fine Art of Charcoal and Gas Outdoor Cooking
BLENDING: The Fine Art of Modern Blending
EGGS: The Fine Art of Egg, Omelet, Soufflé Cooking
PANCAKES & WAFFLES: The Fine Art of Pancakes, Waffles, Crêpe and Blintz Cooking

FROM trp® and DOUBLEDAY of course...

PASTRY APPETIZERS (PAGE 12)   CHOCOLATE FONDUE (PAGE 16)

WOKS AND CHAFING DISHES

SHRIMP AND SNOW PEAS (PAGE 29)   STRAWBERRIES FLAMBÉ (PAGE 54)

INTRODUCTION FONDUE

Guests get acquainted in a hurry at fondue parties. They sit around small tables each with its own fondue pot and relax quickly as they become absorbed in dunking, swirling and cooking tasty bites in a communal pot. The food is eaten and the process repeated as long as food and appetites last.

The cheese fondue is the first and probably the most famous of the fondues. Now there are scores of other favorites, meat, fish and seafood ones, the delicious dessert fondues and an endless number of appetizers, nibblers and snacks. All can be quickly cooked and enjoyed by guests. Here are just a few. Try them all and you'll discover many more.

To help you select recipes which are different and have a foreign flair we have placed this seal next to the title. GOURMET INTERNATIONAL ™

Fondue Bourguignonne

Fondue Bourguignonne, a comparative newcomer, captivates men for it's a way they can enjoy steak cooked the way they like it best.

Bite-size cubes of beef sirloin or tenderloin, condiments, meat sauces and foods for nibbling are grouped around a pot filled with a hot oil and butter combination. Everyone sits around the fondue pot, spearing beef cubes on long handled forks and cooking them in the oil to the doneness desired. It's cooled slightly, dunked in a sauce and popped into the mouth. See recipe for Fondue Bourguignonne on page 8.

WHAT TO SERVE: A dinner or evening party planned around Fondue Bourguignonne is wonderfully easy on the hostess.

The beef, sauces and salad can be prepared ahead of time, covered and refrigerated until serving time and the condiments arranged on serving trays and equipment assembled for easy last minute fixing.

These are some of the foods folks like best with Fondue Bourguignonne. Choose the ones your guests will like best.

Condiments — Catsup or chili sauce, mustard, horseradish, bottled steak sauce, liquid hot red pepper sauce, salt and freshly ground pepper.

Sauces—Bernaise, barbecue, Cumberland, mustard, or horseradish. See Sauces on pages 47, 48 and 49 and What Sauces to Serve? on page 47.

Fresh Vegetable Relishes — Green onions, radishes, celery hearts, cherry tomatoes or slices of cucumber, zucchini, carrot or cauliflower.

Relishes and Pickles — Beet and horseradish corn or hamburger relish; dill, sweet sour or beet and onion pickles; black or stuffed olives; pickled peaches or chutney.

Salads — Caesar, tossed vegetable, coleslaw.

Other Foods — Potato chips, bread sticks or hard rolls, sliced hot buttered French or Italian bread or French fried onion rings.

Beverages—Coffee, tea, if desired, a good (room temperature) Burgundy or chilled rosé wine.

HOW TO SERVE: Assemble Electric Type Fondue or Flame Type Fondue in the center of a small sturdy, tip-proof table for two to four people. If a large party is being given set up as many tables as needed.

Place a sectioned fondue plate, napkin, fork (for eating), long handled fondue fork (for cooking) and a salad fork on the tables for each person. Also place a plate of beef cubes, sauces and a tray of condiments on the table.

Preheat the oil or oil-butter combination in the Electric Type Fondue. The oil in a Flame Type Fondue can be heated on the kitchen range and then transferred to the frame or stand in the center of the serving table. Light the fuel and everything is ready.

CAUTION: When heating oil or oil-butter combination in a Flame Type Fondue on the range start with a low or moderate heat to protect the fondue pot. Increase heat gradually. Never put a cold pot on direct high heat. Never let open flame come in contact with flame guard. Extreme heat will carbonize wooden handles and weaken them so they become dangerous.

Equipment Needed

Before using fondue pot carefully read and follow the instructions for use and care supplied by the manufacturer. The useable capacity of pots varies from about 2½ cups to 8 to 10 cups. Check recipe quantity to make sure it will fit in your unit.

Electric Type Fondue—For Fondue Bourguignonne, Tempura and other foods cooked in extremely hot oil fill base or pot about half full (about 4 cups) with oil or oil-butter combination and preheat about 15 minutes. Electric Type Units automatically maintain the proper oil temperature eliminating guesswork. With Electric Type Units the oil or oil-butter combination is not preheated on the range. With those units that have a choice of heat settings the low temperature is for chocolate or dessert, medium is for cheese and the high is for oil cooking.

Electric Type Thermostats have a variety of descriptions for heat settings. Most of them start in the OFF position and go from the LOW (LO) to the MEDIUM (MED) to the HIGH (HI) range or from number 1 to number 4 for the low to the high range. In some units the spread is from 1 to 10 or 12. Some of the new controls have the heat designated by function such as DESSERT, CHEESE and MEAT or OIL.

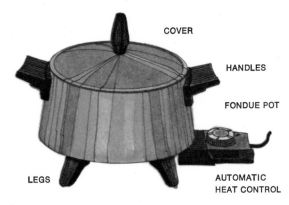

COVER

HANDLES

FONDUE POT

LEGS

AUTOMATIC HEAT CONTROL

Flame Type Fondue—Important: Use a metal fondue pot with sloping sides when cooking with oil. Never use pottery or ceramic pots for oil type cooking! The continued high heat could cause them to crack and break with disastrous results.

CAUTION: Never subject fondue pot to an extreme change in temperature. A shock from heat or cold can warp metal, crack or craze ceramic or porcelain and discolor the finish. Never set a hot pot on a cold, damp or wet surface.

COVER

FLAME GUARD

METAL FONDUE POT

FRAME

TRAY

ALCOHOL BURNER

WICK BURNER

Fondue Forks—Should be at least 9 or 10 inches long and can be either conventional or modern in design. They must have insulated handles of wood or plastic which will remain cool during the cooking process. Two tined forks are for general service but the two tined forks with the barbs are especially designed for meat, the barbs prevent the meat from slipping off the fork into the hot oil. Three and four tined forks are best suited for use in dipping breads and desserts. Forks are available in a great number of handsome styles and colors, you'll want several sets.

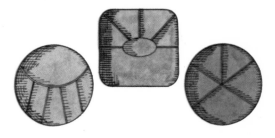

Fondue Plates—Are available in white or colored china, pottery, plastic or metal and with attractive varicolored designs. They are sectioned to keep sauces and other foods separated. Plain or fancy they're designed to please the young hostess with a flair.

Fondue Fuels—Canned heat and alcohol are the principal fuels. Some units use butane and others use electricity. For a complete description of fuels see "Chafing Dish and Fondue Pot Fuels" on page 33.

Seafood and Fish Fondue

Shrimps, scallops and thin strips of fish can be cooked much the same way as beef for Fondue Bourguignonne. See recipe for Fish and Shrimp Fondue on page 8.

The equipment used for cooking fish and seafood fondue is the same as for Fondue Bourguignonne. The accompanying foods are the same except substitute tartar and fish sauces for the steak type sauces and for those liking fresh lemon or lime juice with fish and seafood include citrus wedges on the relish tray.

Cheese Fondue

The Swiss claim the fabulous Cheese Fondue, fortified with dry white wine, is their national dish. In recent years this fine food has become a favorite party dish in America as well as the skiing centers of the world.

The Swiss style Cheese Fondue is said to have been the product of necessity. Everything about it is traditional, the utensils, ingredients and the quaint and friendly method of serving.

Cheese and wine were both important industries in Switzerland in the 18th century and cheese, wine and bread were all readily available in the homes. Some resourceful Swiss cook developed Cheese Fondue and it's been enjoyed ever since.

Traditional Cheese Fondue is really not difficult to make and once the technique is mastered make it the inspiration for lots of easy-do fun and feasting. Serve it for informal occasions as an appetizer, main course or evening party. It's easily prepared, inexpensive and eating it a gay parlor game.

Try the Alpine Cheese Fondue, see page 9, it's fondue connoisseur's of fine foods will like. For those preferring fondue made without wine the Family Style Cheese Fondue on page 10 will please.

Ingredients for Traditional Cheese Fondue

The selection of cheese and wine is most important. A natural well-aged Swiss cheese, domestic or imported, is used unless a mild fondue is desired then Gruyère cheese is substituted for one half of the Swiss. The cheese is shredded or diced very fine and dredged in flour.

The best wines for fondue are the sparkling, light, dry ones such as Neuchâtel, Rhine, Reisling or Chablis.

Traditional Fondues Are Made This Way

The inside of the fondue pot or caquelon is rubbed with garlic. The wine is then added and warmed slowly until tiny bubbles form on the bottom of the pot and rise to the top. Do not allow wine to boil! At this point cheese is added, a handful at a time, and stirring is constant until all cheese is added, melted and bubbling hot.

A dash of nutmeg or mace and pepper and a little kirsch, brandy or cognac is added to give the fondue its distinctive flavor.

Some Precautions

Keep fondue hot with as low a heat as possible to keep it from becoming tough and stringy.

Should fondue become lumpy or the fat tend to separate, return it to a higher heat and beat briskly with a wire whisk or mix 2 tablespoons cornstarch and 1/4 cup wine and stir into fondue. Heat, stirring constantly, until fondue is smooth.

If fondue is too thick it can be thinned to the desired consistency with preheated (never cold) wine. The amount of wine depends upon thickness of fondue. Add wine as needed, a small amount at a time.

How To Serve

Arrange tables for a few or a crowd as suggested for Fondue Bourguignonne (page 4).

Each guest sits around the fondue pot and spears a cube of bread, with crust on one side, with a long handled fondue fork and dips the bread into fondue, giving it a good stir. The bread is lifted out and twirled until cheese stops dripping and cools slightly. The process is repeated as desired.

If desired, halfway through the party small wine glasses half filled with kirsch (cherry brandy) may be served.

After the fondue has been enjoyed and the prized crust on the bottom and edge of the pot is lifted out and eaten serve smoked ham or sausage, crisp relishes, a tempting green salad with an interesting dressing, potato chips and coffee or tea.

If dessert is desired serve chilled fresh, canned or defrosted frozen fruit or simple dessert.

Equipment Needed

Before using fondue pot carefully read and follow the instructions for use and care supplied by the manufacturer. The useable capacity of pots varies from about 2½ cups to 8 to 10 cups. Check recipe quantity to make sure it will fit in your unit.

Fondue plates and forks used for Cheese Fondue are the same as those used for Fondue Bourguignonne, see drawing on page 5.

The cooking utensil for making Cheese Fondue should be the Electric Type Fondue, pottery or ceramic caquelon or a heavy metal pot. These latter type units are available with frame (stand) and flame type burner.

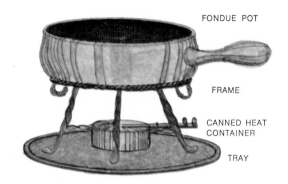

FONDUE POT

FRAME

CANNED HEAT CONTAINER

TRAY

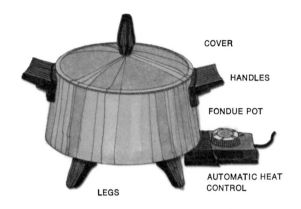

COVER

HANDLES

FONDUE POT

AUTOMATIC HEAT CONTROL

LEGS

Do not subject a pottery or ceramic fondue pot to sudden changes in temperature. Heating or cooling too rapidly can result in cracking or breaking the pot. Never place a hot pot on a cold, damp or wet surface.

Fondue Variations

Tempting fondues can be quickly made once the basic fondue is prepared. See pages 10 and 11 for Flaming, Shrimp, Crab, Lobster, Ham, Mushroom and Tomato Cheese Fondues.

Dessert Fondues

The plates and forks for dessert fondues are the same as those used for Fondue Bourguignonne and Cheese Fondue, see drawings on page 5. Chocolate fondues are made in Electric Type Units or in small ceramic or earthenware pots with a flame type heater or a candle to keep the sauce warm. With care and low heat the larger ceramic or metal type pots can be used.

What Wine To Serve?

WITH	SERVE	
Appetizers and soup	Dry sherry	Chilled slightly
Meat, game, cheese, spaghetti, etc.	Burgundy Claret Red Chianti	Room temperature
	Rosé	Refrigerate 2 to 4 hours
Seafood, chicken, eggs, light entrées, etc.	Sauterne Chablis Rhine wine Reisling Rosé	Refrigerate 2 to 4 hours, never put ice in wine
Desserts, nuts, fruits, cookies	Port White port Muscatel Sweet sherry Madeira	Chilled or at cool room temperature

Oils to Use

For Meats, Fish, Seafood, Poultry, Vegetables, Appetizers, Pastries and Mini-Fried Pies.

A good cooking or salad oil (corn, cottonseed or peanut) is preferred by most. These oils are practically flavorless so are best for preparing foods with their own delicate and distinctive flavor. These oils have high smoking points, are inexpensive and can be strained and reused several times.

Beef fondue fanciers often prefer the flavor of the meat cooked in a mixture of ½ to ¾ cooking oil and ½ to ¼ butter or margarine. The butter or margarine should be clarified, if possible, so there will be a minimum of spattering during frying and no burned milk solid specks collect in cooking oil.

To clarify butter or margarine melt it in a small pan over hot water until milk solids settle to bottom of pan. Skim off any foam. Strain yellow oil through a very fine sieve or several layers of fine mesh cheesecloth into container with tightly fitting cover. Can be refrigerated up to 2 or 3 weeks for later use.

Olive oil is not generally recommended for preparing fried foods because of its low smoking point, its cost and flavor which tends to mask the flavor of the food being cooked. If a small amount of olive oil is desired for flavor add 2 to 4 tablespoons, never more than ¼ of total measure of oil, to the corn, cottonseed or peanut cooking oils being used.

To Reuse Cooking Oil

To clarify oil strain cooled oil through a very fine sieve or several layers of fine mesh cheesecloth. Oil can be stored in a glass container with tight fitting lid and refrigerated for reuse.

Remove strong flavors after frying strong flavored foods by clarifying oil then pour it into a saucepan. Add a few slices of raw potato and reheat oil slowly. Remove potato and discard. Cool oil; strain and store as directed above.

For Cooking	Use
Beef, fish, seafood, poultry, fritters, appetizers, pastries and mini-fried pies	Corn, cottonseed or peanut oil
Beef, fish or seafood fondue and vegetables	The above oils or a mixture of ½ to ¾ cooking oil and ½ to ¼ clarified butter.

FUN-DO FONDUES

Fish and Shrimp Fondue
GOURMET INTERNATIONAL

1 pound slice (½ to ¾ inch) salmon, halibut, or swordfish
1 pound raw shrimp, shelled, deveined, washed, and dried
Cooking oil or half butter and half oil
Favorite fish or seafood sauces (pages 48 and 49)

Cut fish into strips ¼ inch wide and 2 inches long. Refrigerate in covered dish until cooking time. Fill metal fondue pot ½ full with oil, or butter and oil mixture. Heat oil on stove to 350°F. If a butter-oil mixture is used, heat it slowly until butter bubbles and mixture turns a golden color. Place fondue pot on stand over moderately high, direct heat. Loop a fish strip onto a long heavy bamboo skewer. Hold it in hot fat until fish is cooked and lightly browned. Fry shrimp on fondue forks or long bamboo skewers in hot fat until cooked and pink in color. Cool slightly; serve with favorite fish sauce (curry, tartar, seafood, etc.). Yield: 4 to 6 servings. Count on ⅓ pound fish or seafood per serving.

Beef Fondue or Fondue Bourguignonne
GOURMET INTERNATIONAL

See photo on front cover

3-pound piece boneless beef sirloin or tenderloin
Cooking oil, or half butter and half cooking oil
Favorite Meat Sauces (pages 47, 48 and 49)

Trim fat from meat; cut into bite-size cubes. Refrigerate until 20 minutes before cooking time. Fill metal fondue pot about ½ full with oil, or butter and oil mixture. Heat oil on stove to 360°F. If butter-oil mixture is used, heat slowly until butter bubbles and mixture turns a golden color. Set fondue pot on stand over moderately high direct heat and maintain heat. Each guest spears a cube of beef with a fondue fork; holds it in the hot fat until cooked to the doneness desired, 1 to 3 minutes. Remove meat from fork and cool slightly. Serve with favorite meat, barbecue, or Bearnaise sauce. Yield: About 6 servings. Count on ½ pound of meat per adult serving.

Alpine Cheese Fondue
(Made with Wine)

1 clove garlic, cut in half
1/2 pound natural Swiss cheese, shredded
1/2 pound Gruyère, shredded
3 tablespoons flour
2 cups dry white wine (Neuchâtel, Rhine, or
    Chablis)
1 tablespoon lemon juice, optional
Dash of pepper
Dash of nutmeg
2 tablespoons kirsch or cognac
1/8 teaspoon salt, or to taste
French or Italian bread (1 or 2 loaves)

Rub inside surface of ceramic fondue pot with garlic; discard. Toss cheeses with flour. Pour wine into fondue pot; set over low heat. When small bubbles show on bottom and around edge of pot, stir in lemon juice and handfuls of cheese, stirring constantly, after each addition, with wooden spoon until cheese melts. Stir in spices and kirsch or cognac. Serve at once with French or Italian bread cubes cut so each cube has a crust edge. Spear a bread cube with long-handled fondue fork, plunging tines through softened side of cube to crust. Swirl bread cube in cheese mixture; cool slightly before eating. Yield: About 3 cups fondue, 6 to 8 servings.

Quick Cheese Fondue

1 can (10³/₄ ounces) condensed Cheddar
    cheese soup, undiluted
1 cup commercial French onion dip
1 cup shredded sharp Cheddar cheese
    (4 ounces)
1/2 teaspoon dry mustard
2 dashes cayenne pepper
French bread, cut in 1-inch cubes

Combine all ingredients except French bread in fondue pot; mix. Place over low heat until cheese melts and mixture is hot, stirring constantly. To serve turn heat to low. Spear a crust-edged cube of bread with fondue fork and twirl bread in cheese; drain and cool slightly before serving. Yield: 2½ cups, 4 to 6 servings.

Family-Style Swiss Cheese Fondue

3 tablespoons butter or margarine
3 tablespoons flour
$1/2$ teaspoon garlic salt
$1/2$ teaspoon salt
Dash white pepper
Dash nutmeg
$2^{1}/_{2}$ cups milk (scalded, if in a hurry)
1 pound process Swiss cheese, shredded
1 teaspoon Worcestershire sauce
Dash of Tabasco sauce
$1/3$ cup dry white wine (or milk if preferred)
2 tablespoons kirsch (or milk if preferred)
French bread, cut in 1-inch cubes

Melt butter or margarine in ceramic fondue pot over a moderate direct heat. Stir in next 5 ingredients. Stir in milk; cook, stirring constantly until sauce is smooth and thickened slightly. Lower heat. Add cheese, a small amount at a time and stir until cheese is melted after each addition. Stir in remaining ingredients except bread. To serve let each guest spear a crust-edged cube of bread with fondue fork and twirl bread in cheese mixture until coated. Drain, cool, and eat. Yield: About $3^{3}/_{4}$ cups fondue.

Cheese Fondue Variations

Follow recipe for Alpine Cheese or Family-Style Swiss Cheese Fondue and change as follows:

SHRIMP FONDUE: Stir in 1 or 2 cans ($4^{1}/_{2}$ ounce), drained and finely chopped shrimp before serving.

FONDUE WITH HAM OR CANADIAN BACON: Stir in 1 cup finely chopped fully cooked ham or Canadian bacon before serving.

FONDUE WITH MUSHROOMS: Stir in 1 or 2 cans ($4^{1}/_{2}$ ounce) sliced mushrooms, drained, and finely chopped, and 2 teaspoons chopped chives before serving.

FLAMING FONDUE: Pour 3 to 4 tablespoons of kirsch, heated in ladle, over hot fondue. Ignite; serve as soon as flame dies.

Tomato-Cheese Fondue

1 can ($10^{1}/_{2}$ ounce) condensed cream of tomato soup
$2/3$ cup milk
2 teaspoons prepared mustard
1 pound Cheddar cheese, shredded (4 cups)
1 tablespoon chopped chives, optional

Combine first 3 ingredients in ceramic fondue pot over direct, low heat. Heat, stirring often. Sprinkle shredded cheese $1/2$ cup at a time into hot soup; stir after each addition. Stir in chives. Serve as appetizer or main course with French bread cubes, small toast triangles, or bread sticks. Yield: 6 to 8 servings.

Welsh Rarebit

$1^{1}/_{2}$ tablespoons butter or margarine
$1^{1}/_{2}$ tablespoons flour
1 teaspoon salt
$1/2$ teaspoon dry mustard
$1/8$ teaspoon paprika
1 cup milk
$1/2$ teaspoon Worcestershire sauce
2 cups shredded sharp pasteurized cheese
Toast points or toasted English muffins

Melt butter or margarine in metal fondue pot over moderate direct heat. Stir in flour, salt and spices. Stir in milk and Worcestershire sauce. Cook, stirring constantly, until thickened. Turn heat to low. Add cheese; stir constantly until melted. Serve on toast points or toasted English muffins. Yield: 6 servings.

Rinktum Ditty

2 tablespoons butter or margarine
$1/3$ cup finely chopped onion
1 tablespoon flour
$1/2$ teaspoon salt
1 can ($10^{1}/_{2}$ ounce) condensed tomato soup, undiluted
1 teaspoon prepared mustard
$1/2$ teaspoon Worcestershire sauce
3 cups shredded sharp Cheddar cheese (about $3/4$ pound)

Heat butter or margarine in metal fondue pot over moderate direct heat. Add onion and cook, stirring constantly, until onion is limp. Stir in flour and salt, then soup. Heat, stirring often. Reduce heat. Add mustard, Worcestershire sauce and cheese and stir until cheese melts. Serve on toast, plain or topped with tomato slice and bacon curls. Yield: About 3 cups sauce, enough for 6 servings.

Lobster or Crab Fondue Gourmet International

See photo at left

1 can (10 ounce) frozen condensed cream of shrimp soup, defrosted
$1/4$ cup milk or half and half (half milk, half cream)
1 can ($7^1/2$ ounce) lobster or crab meat, drained and flaked
$1/2$ cup shredded process American or Cheddar cheese
2 teaspoons lemon juice
Dash paprika
Dash white pepper
2 tablespoons sherry, optional

Combine first 2 ingredients in metal or ceramic fondue pot. Cover; heat over direct moderate heat, stirring often. Fold in remaining ingredients, except sherry. Heat to serving temperature over direct low heat. If desired, stir in sherry just before serving. Use as an appetizer with Melba toast or as a luncheon dish on toast points or in patty shells. If a thinner mixture is desired, stir in milk or half and half as needed. Yield: About $2^3/4$ cups.

Tempura

See photo back cover

Japanese Tempura is now enjoyed the world around. It's wonderful food for cocktail parties, family and company dinners or late evening party snacks.

Assemble an assortment of foods and **Tempura** Batter. (See Tempura Foods listed on page 12.) Each guest spears a piece of food, dips it into batter, drains well and then holds it in hot oil until lightly browned about 1 to 3 minutes. Drain and dip into Tempura Sauce.

Tempura Batter

2 eggs
$1^3/4$ cups very cold water
$1^3/4$ cups unsifted flour
$1/4$ teaspoon salt, optional

Beat eggs and water until frothy. Beat in flour until batter is smooth. Refrigerate until used. Place batter in bowl in crushed ice to keep cool while using. Yield: About $2^1/2$ cups batter.

Tempura Foods

Raw Shrimp . . . . Shell (leaving tail on), devein, wash and drain.

Lobster Tails . . . . Shell and cut crosswise into ¼-inch slices.

Lean Beef . . . . Cut sirloin or tenderloin into ½-inch cubes.

Fresh Asparagus . . . . Wash; remove tough ends and dry. Cut crosswise into 2-inch lengths.

Celery . . . . Wash and dry stalks. Cut crosswise into 2-inch lengths.

Carrots . . . . Peel and cut crosswise, on the diagonal, into slices ⅛ to ¼-inch thick.

Green or Wax Beans . . . . String, wash and precook 5 minutes. Drain and cut crosswise, on the diagonal, into 2-inch lengths.

Chinese Parsley . . . . Wash, dry and break into **and Watercress** small clusters.

Fresh Mushrooms . . . . . . Wash, dry and cut medium-size mushrooms into halves.

Fresh Chinese Pea Pods . . String, wash and dry.

Green Pepper . . . . Clean and cut in 1-inch squares.

Cauliflower . . . . Clean and break into flowerettes.

Onion . . . . Peel and cut in ½-inch wide strips.

Eggplant . . . . Remove stems, wash and dry. Quarter and cut into slices ¼-inch thick.

Sweet Potato . . . . Peel and cut crosswise into slices ¼-inch thick.

Tempura Sauce

2 cups fish stock or water
1 cup soy sauce
1 cup sake (rice wine), mirim (sweet rice wine) or sherry
Dash of monosodium glutamate

Combine ingredients; bring to a boil. Yield: 4 cups, enough for 6 people.

Foods to Serve With Tempura

Hot cooked seasoned rice
Grated Japanese radish or ⅔ grated red radishes and ⅓ grated turnip
Grated fresh ginger root
Lemon wedges

APPETIZERS

Pastry Appetizers

See photo at right and page 2

1 package (9½ or 10 ounce) pie crust mix
Filling (see pastry suggestions following)
Cooking oil

Prepare pie crust as directed on package label; shape into flat patty. Wrap in foil or plastic film; let stand at room temperature 15 to 20 minutes. Cut patty in half; roll each on lightly floured board to ⅛ inch thickness and into a rectangle 13½ x 9 inches. Cut into 2¼ inch squares. Center desired filling on pastry. Moisten edges; bring 4 corners together in center; seal edges well. Arrange on tray; cover and chill until ready to fry. At serving time fill metal fondue pot ½ full with oil; heat to 350°F. on stove. Place on stand over direct high heat and maintain temperature. Plunge a fondue fork or a long heavy bamboo skewer clear through pastry. Cook in hot fat until done and lightly browned, about 5 minutes. Remove from fork or skewer; cool slightly. Yield: 1 package crust makes 24 to 36 appetizers.

Pastry Appetizer Variations

Prepare appetizers as suggested above using one of the following fillings:

CHEESE-ONION PASTRIES: Center a ¾ x ¾ x ⅛-inch cheese slice on crust and top with a small pickled or cocktail onion.

CHEESE-OLIVE PASTRIES: Prepare same as Cheese-Onion Pastries and substitute a stuffed olive for onion.

GINGER HAM PASTRIES: Spoon ½ teaspoon Ginger Ham Balls mixture (page 13) in center of pastry squares.

LIVER SAUSAGE PASTRIES: Spoon ½ teaspoon liver sausage in center of each pastry square.

Chafing Dish Appetizers

Tempting appetizers that are easily prepared in chafing dish, crêpe suzette or blazer pan can be found on pages 34 and 36. All are crowd pleasers!

A—SPICY BEEF EMPANADAS
B—PASTRY APPETIZERS (PAGE 12)
C—CRUSTY FRANK SNACKS (PAGE 14)
D—GINGER HAM BALLS

Spicy Beef Empanadas

See photo at left

1 teaspoon butter or margarine
$1/2$ pound lean ground beef
$1/2$ cup chopped onion
$1/2$ cup chopped fresh tomatoes
$1/4$ cup chopped pitted black olives
1 tablespoon flour
$1/4$ cup catsup or chili sauce
$1/2$ teaspoon oregano, or to taste
$1/2$ teaspoon chili powder
$1/4$ teaspoon salt
$1/4$ teaspoon garlic salt
6 drops hot pepper sauce
2 packages ($9^1/2$ or 10 ounce) pie crust mix

Melt butter or margarine in heavy fry pan. Add beef and onion; cook, stirring until beef is crumbly and onion soft. Stir in remaining ingredients, except pie crust mix. Cook slowly until thickened, about 10 minutes, stirring often. Chill well. While meat is chilling prepare pie crust mix as directed on package label. Roll, cut crust, fill, store, and cook as directed for Mini Fried Fruit Pies (page 18) using Spicy Beef filling. Yield: About 48 appetizer-size empanadas.

Ginger Ham Balls

See photo at left

$1^1/2$ pounds ground fully cooked ham
$1/3$ cup fine corn flake or bread crumbs
$1/4$ cup orange marmalade
1 egg, beaten
2 tablespoons finely chopped onion
1 tablespoon finely chopped preserved ginger
1 tablespoon preserved ginger syrup
1 teaspoon soy sauce
Cooking oil

Combine ingredients except oil; mix well. Shape into 1-inch balls, using a rounded teaspoonful of mixture for each ball. Refrigerate until ready to cook. Fill metal fondue pot about $1/2$ full with oil. Heat oil on stove to 350°F. Set fondue pot on stand over direct high heat and maintain temperature. Each guest spears a ham ball with a fondue fork or long heavy bamboo skewer and holds it in the hot oil until ham ball is well browned and done, about $1^1/2$ minutes. Serve as appetizer or entrée. Yield: 3 cups mixture. Makes about 8 dozen balls. Allow 4 to 6 balls per appetizer serving, 8 to 12 balls per entrée serving.

Crusty Frank Snacks

See photo page 13

Open 1 package (8 ounce) refrigerated crescent rolls; separate rolls. Cut each triangular roll into 4 small triangles by cutting in half crosswise through middle; cut bottom half into 3 equal triangles. Put a small, well-drained dollop of hot dog relish in center of each triangle. Top with a miniature cocktail-size, fully cooked frank or wiener. Wrap dough around 2/3 of frank and stick a long bamboo skewer through dough and frank, leaving one side of frank uncovered and ends of dough unskewered. Fry until done and browned, about 2 minutes, in metal fondue pot 1/2 full of hot oil (350°F.) over direct, high heat. Drain. Cool slightly and eat. Yield: 32 appetizers.

Dip Sticks

Open 1 package (8 ounce) refrigerated biscuits; cut crosswise into strips 1/4 inch wide. Fry as directed for Tiny Doughnuts (page 17). Serve with a favorite dip. Yield: About 60 sticks.

Batter Fried Shrimp

Reduce sugar in recipe for Fritter Batter for Fruits (page 20) to 1 tablespoon; substitute seasoned salt for salt and add 1/2 teaspoon chili powder. Spear cooked, shelled, deveined, medium-size shrimp with a fondue fork or long bamboo skewer. Dip shrimp into batter; drain well and lower into hot oil (350°F.). Cook and brown, 3 to 4 minutes; drain. Cool slightly and serve plain or dip into favorite tartar or seafood sauce. Yield: Batter for 25 to 30 shrimp.

COCKTAIL HOT DOGS OR FRANKS: Prepare as for Batter Fried Shrimp (above) substituting cocktail-size, fully cooked franks for cooked shrimp. Serve plain or dip into favorite horseradish or barbecue sauce. Yield: Batter for 20 to 24 cocktail-size franks.

Bagna Cauda

See photo at right

1 cup soft butter or margarine
1/3 cup olive or peanut oil
3 small garlic cloves, slivered
1 or 2 cans (2 ounce) anchovy fillets, well drained
Bagna Cauda Vegetables (allow 1/2 to 1 cup vegetables per person)
French or Italian bread, cut in 1/4-inch slices

Combine first 4 ingredients in blender; whiz just until anchovies and garlic pieces are finely chopped. If no blender is available, mince garlic and finely chop anchovies. Pour into ceramic, metal or electric fondue pot; heat slowly over direct flame or medium heat until mixture is bubbly. Turn flame or heat to low; keep just hot enough to heat and lightly brown vegetables without burning. To serve spear a vegetable piece with a fondue fork or long heavy bamboo skewer and swirl vegetable in butter mixture until hot and lightly browned, do not cook. Hold a piece of bread under vegetable as it is removed from fat to catch flavorful drippings. Yield: About 1 1/2 cups sauce, enough for 5 to 6 cups vegetables, appetizer servings for 10 to 12.

Bagna Cauda Vegetables

Choose an assortment of any of the following:

CARROTS: peel and cut crosswise into 1/2 inch slices.

CAULIFLOWER: clean and break into flowerettes.

GREEN BEANS: clean, stem and dry.

CHERRY TOMATOES: wash and dry.

GREEN OR RED PEPPERS: clean and cut lengthwise into 1/2 inch strips.

MUSHROOMS: clean, dry, leave whole or cut in half.

ZUCCHINI: wash, dry and cut crosswise into 1/2 inch slices.

BAGNA CAUDA (PAGE 14)

DESSERTS

Chocolate Fondue

GOURMET INTERNATIONAL™

See photo page 2

2 tablespoons honey or light corn syrup
1/2 cup light cream or half and half (half milk,
    half cream)
1 bar (8³/4 or 9 ounce) milk chocolate, broken
    into small pieces
1/4 cup very finely chopped toasted almonds or
    pecans, optional
1 teaspoon vanilla
2 tablespoons Cointreau, optional
Foods for twirling (at right)

Heat honey and cream or half and half in ceramic or metal fondue pot over direct high
heat. Lower heat; stir in chocolate pieces.
Heat, stirring constantly, until chocolate is
melted. Stir in nuts, vanilla and Cointreau, if
used. Let guests spear favorite foods for twirling
with fondue fork and swirl in chocolate mixture. Cool slightly and eat. Yield: About 1¹/2
cups sauce.

CHOCOLATE MINT FONDUE: Follow recipe for
Chocolate Fondue (above) and change as follows. Omit nuts. Substitute 1/4 teaspoon mint
extract for vanilla and use crème de menthe instead of Cointreau. Yield: About 1¹/2 cups.

CHOCOLATE RUM FONDUE: Follow recipe for
Chocolate Fondue (above) and change as follows. Omit nuts if desired. Substitute 1/4 to 1/2
teaspoon rum extract for vanilla and light or
dark rum for Cointreau. Yield: About 1¹/2 cups.

Foods for Twirling in Chocolate Fondue

Choose an assortment of any of the following:

CAKE: Bite-size chunks of angel food, pound,
sponge, or chocolate cake

APPLES: Peeled and cut into wedges

BANANAS: Cut crosswise into bite-size slices

CANTALOUPE OR HONEYDEW MELON:
Peeled, seeded, cut into bite-size pieces and
drained on paper toweling

CANNED, SLICED PINEAPPLE: Drained on paper toweling and quartered

FRESH PEACHES OR NECTARINES: Peeled, cut
into bite-size chunks or slices, and drained on
paper toweling

FRESH PINEAPPLE: Peeled, cored, cubed, and
drained

FRESH STRAWBERRIES: Stemmed, washed, and
dried

ORANGE SECTIONS: Dried on paper toweling

SEEDLESS GRAPES: Washed and dried

LADYFINGERS

MARSHMALLOWS

POPCORN

UNFROSTED BROWNIE BITES

Sugared Puffs

Fill metal fondue pot ½ full with cooking oil. Heat to 350°F. on stove. Transfer to fondue stand and maintain heat over direct high heat. Prepare puffs while oil is heating. Open 1 package (8 ounce) refrigerated crescent rolls. Unroll; separate into triangles. Cut each triangle in half across center and cut bottom half of each into 3 triangles. Cut a ½-inch slit in center of each triangle. Pull point of triangle through slit. Plunge a long heavy bamboo skewer through dough and hold it in hot fat until done and browned, about 2 minutes. Roll in confectioners' or cinnamon sugar while hot, or twirl in Hot Fudge or Peanut Butterscotch Sauce (pages 22, 23). Eat while warm. Yield: 32 puffs.

Tiny Doughnuts

Open 1 package (8 ounce) refrigerated biscuits. Cut each biscuit into quarters; press a hole in the center of each triangle with finger or pointed end of wooden spoon handle. Fry until done and brown in metal fondue pot filled ½ full with hot oil (350°F.) over direct high heat. Drain and sprinkle generously with confectioners' or cinnamon sugar while warm. Yield: 40 tiny doughnut bites.

Chocolate Butterscotch Fondue

  ⅓ cup light cream or half and half
      (half milk, half cream)
  1 tablespoon sugar
  ¼ teaspoon salt
1½ cups semi-sweet chocolate bits
  ½ cup butterscotch bits
  ½ teaspoon vanilla
  ½ teaspoon maple flavoring, optional
Foods for Twirling (page 16)

Heat cream or half and half, sugar and salt in ceramic or metal fondue pot over direct high heat. Lower heat; stir in chocolate and butterscotch bits. Reduce heat to low and allow bits to melt, stirring constantly. Stir in flavorings. Spear wedges of apple, cake squares, doughnut chunks, large marshmallows or other Foods for Twirling and swirl in mixture. Drain and roll in finely chopped nuts, if desired. Yield: About 2⅓ cups.

Apricot Topper

Pour 1 can (1 pound) apricot halves into metal fondue pot; add 1 slice (¼-inch) unpeeled orange, quartered, and 3 or 4 whole cloves. Place over direct high heat. Bring to simmering stage. If desired, add 2 tablespoons apricot or orange flavored liqueur just before serving. Ladle into dessert dishes and top each serving with a dollop of whipped cream or serve on vanilla or French vanilla ice cream. Yield: Fruit for about 4 desserts.

Hot Cherry Topper

Pour 1 can (1 pound) pitted Bing or sweetened red cherries into fondue pot. Place over direct high heat. Bring to simmering stage. Stir in 1 or 2 tablespoons Cointreau or other orange flavored liqueur, if desired. Ladle over vanilla or New York ice cream. Top with a dollop of whipped cream or dessert topping. Yield: Fruit for 4 to 6 desserts.

Orange Marmalade Fondue

3 tablespoons butter or margarine
3 tablespoons sugar
1 tablespoon flour
1/2 cup whipping cream
1/3 cup orange marmalade
1/2 teaspoon grated orange rind
2 tablespoons orange liqueur (Cointreau or Grand Marnier), optional

Heat butter or margarine in ceramic or metal fondue pot over low heat; stir in mixture of sugar and flour. Stir in cream; cook slowly, stirring often. Stir in marmalade, orange rind, and liqueur, if desired. Use as dip for pineapple or banana chunks, or cake squares. Yield: About 1 cup.

Pears Helene

6 chilled canned pear halves
2 pint bricks vanilla or mint ice cream
Hot Fudge Sauce (page 22)
Whipped cream or dessert topping

Drain pears well. Cut each pint of ice cream into 3 even slices. Place slices on freezer chilled dessert plates. Top each ice cream slice with a pear half; serve with Hot Fudge Sauce and top with whipped cream or dessert topping. Yield: 6 servings.

Peach Melba Cake Squares

1 package (10 ounce) frozen red raspberries, partially frozen
1/2 cup currant jelly
1/4 cup sugar
1 tablespoon cornstarch
2 tablespoons water
6 thick slices (3/4-inch) pound cake
6 large well-drained canned peach halves

Combine and heat first 3 ingredients in metal fondue pot over moderate direct heat. Mix cornstarch and water until free of lumps. Stir into fruit mixture and cook, stirring constantly, until mixture thickens. Top each cake slice with a peach half, cavity side up. Spoon sauce over peaches and serve. Yield: 6 servings.

Mini Fried Fruit Pies

See photo at right

1 package (9 1/2 or 10 ounce) pie crust mix
1/2 to 3/4 cup filling (below)
Cooking oil
Confectioners' sugar

Prepare pie crust as directed on package label; shape into flat patty. Wrap in foil or plastic film; let stand at room temperature 15 to 20 minutes. Roll dough on lightly floured board to 1/8-inch thickness. Cut into 2 3/4 inch rounds with floured cookie cutter. Spoon 1 teaspoon favorite filling to one side of center on each pastry round. Moisten crust edges; fold in half, seal and flute edges with tines of dinner fork. Place on tray; cover and chill until ready to fry. At serving time fill metal fondue pot 1/2 full with oil; heat on stove to 350°F. Place on fondue stand over direct high heat; maintain temperature. Let guests spear a pie at a time with a fondue fork or long heavy bamboo skewer, pushing point clear through pie. Lower into hot fat; cook until done and lightly browned, about 5 minutes. Remove from skewer; dust with confectioners' sugar. Cool slightly before eating. Yield: 1 package crust will make 24 to 36 pies. About 1/2 to 3/4 cup filling will be required.

Quick, Easy Filling For Mini Fried Fruit Pies

APPLE: Use canned apple-pie filling. Use well-drained apple pieces for filling pies; save leftover sauce to serve with hot pies, if desired.

APRICOT OR PRUNE: Use one of the commercial canned apricot or prune fillings for cake or pastry.

CHERRY: Same as for apple.

MINCEMEAT: Use well-drained or thick, canned mincemeat.

MINI FRIED FRUIT PIES (PAGE 18)

Fritter Batter For Fruits

See photo at right

1 cup sifted flour
3 tablespoons sugar
1^1/$_2$ teaspoons baking powder
^{1}/$_2$ teaspoon salt
2 eggs, beaten
^{1}/$_3$ cup milk
1 tablespoon oil, melted butter or margarine

Sift first 4 ingredients into bowl. Add remaining ingredients; stir until smooth or whiz all ingredients in blender at low speed until smooth. Use for making favorite fruit fritters. Yield: About 1^1/$_3$ cups batter.

BANANA FRITTER BITES *(See photo at right):* Prepare Fritter Batter for Fruits (recipe above). Fill metal fondue pot ^{1}/$_2$ full with cooking oil. Heat on stove to 350°F. Place pot on fondue stand over direct high heat and maintain temperature. Cut bananas crosswise into 1 or 1¼ inch slices. Spear a banana slice with fondue fork. Dip into Fritter Batter for Fruits; drain well and hold in hot oil until a golden brown on all sides, 2 to 3 minutes. Cool slightly; dip into confectioners' sugar; remove from fork. Eat and fry another. Yield: Batter for 36 to 40 fritters.

FRITTER BATTER FOR FRUITS

STRAWBERRY FRITTERS *(See photo at left):* Prepare as for Banana Fritter Bites (page 20) and substitute whole, washed, dried, and stemmed strawberries for banana slices. Yield: Enough batter for about 1 pint strawberries.

BITE-SIZE APPLE FRITTERS *(See photo at left):* Add $1/8$ teaspoon cinnamon to Fritter Batter for Fruits (page 20). Heat oil as directed for Banana Fritters. Cut 4 to 5 small, peeled, and cored apples crosswise into $1/2$-inch thick slices. Cut slices into thirds or quarters. To keep apple pieces from darkening, drizzle 1 tablespoon lemon juice over apples; mix. Spear an apple piece with a long-handled fondue fork. Dip into batter; drain well. Hold in hot oil until golden brown on all sides, $1\frac{1}{2}$ to 2 minutes. Cool slightly; dip in confectioners' or cinnamon sugar. Remove from fork, eat and fry another. Yield: Batter for 36 to 40 fritters.

More Fun-Do Desserts

See pages 55, 56, and 57 for recipes for Cherries Jubilee and fruit dumplings, quick and easy chafing dish desserts which can be made in the larger size (2 to $2\frac{1}{2}$ quart) metal fondue pots equipped with covers.

Dessert Pancakes, Crêpes, and Blintzes

Fancy dessert pancakes, crêpes, and blintzes that will please and amaze guests and family. See pages 50-53 for recipes.

DESSERT SAUCES AND SYRUPS

Sauces and Syrups can only be made in units with adjustable heat control.

Brandied Peach Sauce

1 package (10 or 12 ounce) frozen sliced
  peaches, defrosted
$1/4$ cup sugar
1 tablespoon cornstarch
Dash of salt
$1/2$ cup water
1 tablespoon butter or margarine
2 tablespoons apricot brandy, optional

Drain peaches, save syrup. Combine sugar, cornstarch, and salt in metal fondue pot; mix. Stir in peach syrup and water. Place on stand over direct high heat and cook, stirring constantly, until sauce thickens and clears. Stir in butter or margarine. Fold in peach slices and heat. Fold in brandy, if used. Serve hot on pancakes, waffles, cake slices, or ice cream. Yield: About $1\frac{2}{3}$ cups.

Sauce Variations

Follow recipe for Brandied Peach Sauce and change as suggested below:

RASPBERRY SAUCE: Substitute 1 package (10 ounce) frozen raspberries for peaches. Omit brandy and substitute rum, if desired. Yield: About $1\frac{2}{3}$ cups.

STRAWBERRY SAUCE: Substitute 1 package (10 ounce) frozen sliced strawberries for peaches. Omit brandy. Yield: About $1\frac{2}{3}$ cups.

Hot Fudge Sauce

See photo at left

¹/₂ cup undiluted evaporated milk
1 package (6 ounce) semisweet chocolate bits
1 cup miniature marshmallows
¹/₄ teaspoon salt
1¹/₂ teaspoons vanilla

Heat milk in metal fondue pot over direct moderate heat until bubbles form in milk around edge of pot. Stir in chocolate bits, marshmallows, and salt. Cook, stirring constantly, until chocolate and marshmallows melt. Heat to desired serving temperature, stirring constantly. Remove from heat; stir in vanilla. Serve on ice cream, puddings, cake, or brownie squares. Yield: About 1¹/₃ cups sauce.

Mocha Fudge Sauce

Prepare Hot Fudge Sauce (above) and add 2 to 3 teaspoons instant coffee powder to milk before heating. Yield: About 1¹/₃ cups.

Apricot Rum Sauce

Combine 1 jar (12 ounce) apricot preserves, 3 tablespoons orange juice in metal fondue pot over low direct heat. Heat, stirring often. Stir in 2 tablespoons light rum. Spoon an additional 2 tablespoons light rum over sauce; ignite. Spoon onto cake slices or ice cream when flame dies. Yield: About 1¹/₃ cups sauce.

Maple Walnut Sauce

Pour 1½ cups maple or maple-blended syrup into metal fondue pot over moderate direct heat. Bring to simmering stage; simmer 3 minutes. Add ²/₃ cup coarsely chopped walnuts to syrup. Serve warm or cold on ice cream. Yield: About 2 cups sauce.

HOT FUDGE SAUCE

More Sauce Variations

Follow recipe for Hot Fudge Sauce on page 22 and change as suggested below:

MILK CHOCOLATE SAUCE: Substitute 1 package (5¾ ounce) milk chocolate bits for semisweet ones.

CHOCOLATE MINT SAUCE: Substitute 1 package (6 ounce) mint flavored chocolate bits for semisweet ones.

CHOCOLATE RUM SAUCE: Stir 2 or 3 tablespoons rum into sauce.

CHOCOLATE ORANGE SAUCE: Stir ½ teaspoon grated orange rind and 2 to 3 tablespoons Cointreau into sauce, if desired.

PEANUT-BUTTERSCOTCH SAUCE: Substitute 1 package (6 ounce) butterscotch bits for semisweet chocolate bits. Use ½ cup instead of 1 cup of marshmallows; stir in ¼ cup peanut butter and, if desired, ¼ cup chopped peanuts. Yield: About 1¼ cups sauce.

HOT BUTTERSCOTCH-MALLOW SAUCE: Substitute 1 package (6 ounce) butterscotch bits for semisweet chocolate ones and 1 jar (7 ounce) marshmallow crème for miniature marshmallows. Reduce vanilla to 1 teaspoon and add ½ teaspoon maple flavoring, if desired. Yield: About 1⅓ cups.

Peppermint Patty Sundae Sauce

½ pound chocolate covered peppermint
  patties, cut into quarters or small pieces
2 tablespoons half and half (half milk, half
  cream), cream or undiluted evaporated milk
½ teaspoon peppermint extract or vanilla,
  as desired

Combine candy and half and half, cream or evaporated milk in ceramic fondue pot. Heat over direct moderate heat, stirring constantly, until mixture is smooth. Stir in flavoring. Delicious used as a dessert fondue or as a sundae sauce on ice cream, cake or cream puffs. Yield: About 1 cup.

Sherried Fruit Sundae Sauce

1 cup undrained canned mincemeat
¼ cup coarsely chopped maraschino or
  candied cherries
¼ cup coarsely chopped walnuts or pecans
3 to 4 tablespoons sherry (or fruit brandy)

Combine first 3 ingredients in metal fondue pot; mix. Place on fondue stand over direct moderate heat, stirring constantly. Remove from heat and stir in sherry (or brandy). Serve hot on cake or ice cream. Yield: About 1⅔ cups.

Praline Sauce

1 cup (packed) brown sugar
½ cup light corn syrup
¼ cup water
1 teaspoon cornstarch
Dash salt
½ cup chopped pecans
1 tablespoon butter or margarine

Combine first 5 ingredients in metal fondue pot; mix. Place on fondue stand over direct high heat. Cook, stirring constantly, until sauce thickens and clears. Stir in nuts and butter or margarine. Lower heat and keep warm. Ladle over sliced cake, waffles, or ice cream. Yield: About 1½ cups.

Pineapple Sundae Sauce

1 can (8½ ounce) crushed pineapple
¾ cup light corn syrup
3 tablespoons sugar
Dash salt
1 tablespoon grated orange rind, optional

Drain pineapple well; save juice. Combine pineapple juice, corn syrup, sugar, and salt in metal fondue pot; mix. Place on fondue stand over direct high heat. Cook until bubbles form in mixture in center of pot, stirring until sugar dissolves. Cook slowly until syrup thickens to consistency of thick syrup, about 10 minutes, stirring often. Stir in pineapple and orange rind. Serve hot on ice cream, pancakes, waffles. Yield: About 1¼ cups.

Hot Spiced Applesauce

1 can (16 or 17 ounce) applesauce
1/2 cup maple-flavored pancake syrup
1/2 teaspoon cinnamon
Dash of cloves

Combine ingredients in ceramic or metal fondue pot; mix. Heat over direct high heat, stirring often. Lower heat; keep warm for serving. Ladle onto plain or potato pancakes or waffles. Yield: About 2 1/2 cups.

Orange-Maple Sauce

1/4 cup butter or margarine
1 tablespoon flour
1/4 cup (packed) light brown sugar
1/4 cup water
1/4 cup maple-flavored pancake syrup
1/4 cup orange juice
1 teaspoon grated orange rind
2 tablespoons sherry, optional

Melt butter or margarine in metal fondue pot over direct high heat. Stir in flour and sugar; heat until bubbly. Stir in remaining ingredients, except sherry. Heat; simmer 2 or 3 minutes. Stir in sherry, if used. Ladle over pancakes or waffles. Yield: About 1 1/4 cups.

Quick Caramel Sauce

Combine 1/2 pound commercial vanilla caramels and 1/2 cup milk in metal or ceramic fondue pot. Heat over direct moderate heat and stir until caramels melt and sauce is smooth. Remove from heat; stir in 1/4 teaspoon maple flavoring or 1/2 teaspoon vanilla. Serve hot on cake or ice cream. Yield: About 1 cup.

Quick Caramel Nut Sauce

Prepare Quick Caramel Sauce and fold 1/3 to 1/2 cup of coarsely chopped pecans, walnuts or peanuts into sauce before serving. Yield: About 1 1/3 cups.

Brandy Cranberry Sauce

2 tablespoons cornstarch
3 tablespoons water
1 1/2 cups whole cranberry sauce, canned or homemade
1/2 teaspoon grated orange rind
1/4 cup kirsch, Cointreau or brandy

Combine cornstarch and water; mix well. Add all ingredients, except liqueur, in metal fondue pot; mix well and heat over moderate direct heat, stirring constantly, until thickened. Stir in liqueur. Serve warm on plain or ice cream topped waffles or ice cream. Yield: About 1 3/4 cups sauce.

More Syrups and Sauces

Brandied Peach, Raspberry, and Strawberry sauces (page 21) or Praline Sauce (page 23) are easy elegant fun-do toppings for pancakes, crêpes, and waffles.

Hot Spiced Honey-Butter

1/2 cup butter or margarine
1/4 teaspoon cinnamon
1/8 teaspoon nutmeg
1/2 cup honey

Melt butter or margarine in ceramic or metal fondue pot over direct high heat. Stir in spices and honey; heat. Remove pot from heat; stir vigorously until well blended. Lower heat; keep warm. Ladle over hot cakes or waffles. Yield: About 1 cup.

Hot Orange Honey-Butter

1/4 cup butter or margarine
1/2 cup honey
1/2 cup thick orange marmalade

Melt butter or margarine in ceramic or metal fondue pot over direct high heat. Stir in honey and marmalade; mix and heat. Lower heat; keep warm. Ladle over hot cakes or waffles. Yield: About 1 1/4 cups.

QUICK LUNCH OR SUPPER DISHES

Spaghetti with Hot Dogs

1 can (15¼ ounce) spaghetti in tomato sauce
  with cheese
½ pound fully cooked hot dogs, sliced
1 can (2 ounce) sliced mushrooms, drained
¼ cup chopped green pepper, optional
½ cup shredded Cheddar cheese
½ to ¾ teaspoon oregano, optional

Combine ingredients in metal fondue pot; mix. Cover and heat to serving temperature over direct, moderate heat, stirring often. Yield: 3 to 4 servings.

Meaty Beans

2 cans (1 pound) pork and beans
1 can (12 ounce) luncheon meat, diced
¼ cup catsup
2 tablespoons brown sugar
2 tablespoons sweet pickle relish
1 tablespoon instant minced onion
1 teaspoon prepared mustard

Prepare as directed for Spaghetti with Hot Dogs, above. Yield: 4 to 6 servings.

Chili with Franks

2 cans (15 ounce) chili with or without beans
1 cup tomato juice
½ pound fully-cooked franks, sliced
2 tablespoons instant minced onion
1 teaspoon chili powder

Prepare as directed for Spaghetti with Hot Dogs above. Serve plain or topped with shredded Cheddar cheese. Yield: About 5 cups, 4 to 6 servings.

Speedy Sausage 'N Macaroni

2 cans (15 ounce) macaroni with cheese sauce
2 cans (4 to 5 ounce) Vienna sausages, drained
  and cut in thirds, crosswise
½ cup shredded Cheddar cheese
½ teaspoon prepared mustard
½ teaspoon Worcestershire sauce

Prepare as directed for Spaghetti with Hot Dogs, (at left) Yield: 4 to 6 servings.

French Green Pea Soup, Jiffy-Made

1 can (11¼ ounce) condensed green pea soup
1 soup can milk
1 can (4 ounce) mushroom stems and pieces,
  drained
¾ cup drained, canned, or cooked diced
  carrots
1 teaspoon instant minced onion

Prepare as directed for Spaghetti with Hot Dogs, (at left). Yield: About 3¼ cups, 3 to 4 servings.

Jiffy Beef Stew with Dumplings

1 can (1½ pound) beef stew
1 cup drained cooked mixed vegetables, leftover or canned
1 cup tomato juice or 1 can (8 ounce) tomato
  sauce
2 tablespoons instant minced onion
1 cup prepared biscuit mix
⅓ cup milk

Combine first 4 ingredients in metal fondue pot; mix. Place on fondue stand over direct high heat. Cover; heat to serving temperature, stirring often. Stir biscuit mix and milk with fork until dry ingredients are moistened. Drop 6 spoonfuls of biscuit mix onto hot stew. Cover; turn heat to moderate and cook until dumplings are done, about 15 minutes. Yield: 2 to 3 servings.

MULLED WINE (PAGE 27)

BEVERAGES

Hot Buttered Rum

2 cups boiling water
1 cup dark rum
1¹/₂ tablespoons sugar
4 teaspoons butter or margarine
1 teaspoon Angostura bitters
6 whole cloves

Pour boiling water into large metal fondue pot over direct high heat; bring to a boil. Lower heat; stir in remaining ingredients. Bring to a boil; turn heat off. Let mixture stand 2 or 3 minutes and ladle into heavy mugs. Yield: About 3 to 4 servings.

Hot Spiced Cider

6 cups cider or apple juice*
2 small cinnamon sticks
8 to 10 whole cloves
¹/₄ teaspoon grated orange rind
Small orange slices

Combine ingredients, except orange slices, in metal fondue pot. Heat to serving temperature over direct moderate heat. Ladle hot punch into mugs; top each with an orange slice. Yield: About 6 servings.

*2 cups sauterne may be substituted for 2 cups of the cider or apple juice, if desired.

Hot Chocolate

2¹/₂ cups milk
¹/₂ cup semisweet or milk chocolate bits
1 tablespoon sugar
Dash of salt
1 teaspoon vanilla
Marshmallows, optional

Scald milk in metal fondue pot over direct moderate heat. Add sugar, salt, and a few chocolate bits at a time. Stir until bits are melted. Heat to desired serving temperature, stirring often. Stir in vanilla. Ladle into mugs or cups and top with marshmallows, if desired. Yield: About 2³/₄ cups, 4 servings.

Café Brûlot

2 tablespoons sugar
1 teaspoon grated orange rind
4 whole cloves
2 small cinnamon sticks, broken in half
3 tablespoons brandy
4 cups strong hot black coffee

Combine first 5 ingredients in metal fondue pot or blazer pan of chafing dish. Place over low direct heat. Ignite brandy and let it burn 2 to 4 minutes, stirring constantly with long handled spoon. Add coffee gradually, stirring constantly, until flame dies. Ladle into demitasse cups at once. Yield: Makes about 8 to 10 servings.

Mulled Wine

See photo at left

1 small cinnamon stick, broken into 1-inch pieces
¹/₄ teaspoon ground cloves
¹/₄ teaspoon nutmeg
¹/₄ cup lemon juice
²/₃ cup sugar
1 bottle (4/5 quart) favorite dry red wine (Burgundy or Beaujolais)
1 cup port wine
Thin lemon slices

Combine ingredients except lemon slices in metal fondue pot. Heat to serving temperature over direct moderate heat. To serve, ladle into small mugs or punch cups and top with a lemon slice. Yield: About 8 servings.

CHINESE WOK COOKING

Good Chinese cooks do wonderfully appealing things with food. All do some form of chow or stir-fry cooking in a wok, a round bottom pan that fits into a ring for use over direct heat.

Stir-fry cooking in the wok is fast! Bite-size pieces of food are stirred in a mite of hot oil while being fried in a wok or heavy fry pan.

Try cooking in a wok the stir-fry way. It's fun and you will be amazed at the handsome appearance and magnificent flavor of cooked foods.

Oriental Beef with Vegetables

1½ pounds beef sirloin or tenderloin, ½ to ¾-inch thick
1 small clove garlic, minced
½ cup water
⅓ cup soy sauce
¼ cup cooking oil
1 green pepper, cleaned and cut into thin slices, lengthwise
1 cup thinly sliced celery
2 medium (2-inch) onions, thinly sliced
2 cups thinly sliced celery cabbage
1 can (6 ounce) water chestnuts, drained and thinly sliced
2 cans (4 ounce) sliced mushrooms, drained
1½ tablespoons cornstarch
1 can (8 ounce) tomato juice (1 cup)

Chill meat in freezer until partially frozen, it makes slicing easier. Cut meat across the grain into very thin (⅛-inch) slices; place meat in bowl. Combine garlic, water and soy sauce; pour over meat and mix. Cover; refrigerate 45 minutes to 1 hour. Drain meat; save marinade. Pat meat dry on paper toweling. Heat oil in Chinese wok or in blazer pan of chafing dish over direct high flame. Fry and brown meat pieces quickly, stirring constantly. Add next 6 ingredients; stir and fry just until vegetables are tender yet crisp, 3 to 4 minutes. Combine cornstarch, remaining marinade, and tomato juice; stir until smooth and add to vegetables. Stir until mixture thickens. Serve with Fluffy White Rice (page 46). Yield: 4 to 6 servings.

Stir-fry (Chow) Asparagus

2 tablespoons cooking oil
3 cups bias sliced (½-inch thick and 1¼ inches long) fresh or defrosted, drained, frozen asparagus
¾ teaspoon salt
¼ teaspoon sugar
Dash pepper

Heat oil in Chinese wok, on ring or stand, or blazer pan of chafing dish, or in heavy fry pan on table top butane unit, over direct high flame for about 30 seconds. Lower flame if oil begins to smoke. Swirl oil around edges of pan using wooden spoon. Add asparagus and seasonings. Lower flame and stir and fry just until asparagus is tender but retains a crispness, about 5 minutes. Serve at once. Yield: 4 to 6 servings.

Shrimp Chow Mein

1 pound raw shrimp, shelled, deveined, washed
¼ cup cooking oil
2 cups thin bias-sliced celery
1 small green pepper, cleaned and cut lengthwise into thin strips
1 can (4 ounce) bamboo shoots, drained and thinly sliced
1 can (1 pound) bean sprouts, drained
2 cans (4 ounce) button mushrooms, drained
1 can (13½ ounce) chicken bouillon
¾ teaspoon salt
¼ teaspoon garlic salt
¼ teaspoon onion salt
2 tablespoons soy sauce
2 tablespoons cornstarch
¼ cup cold water
chow mein noodles

Dry shrimp on paper toweling. Heat oil in Chinese wok or in blazer pan of chafing dish over direct high flame. Add shrimp; stir and fry until shrimp is cooked and turns pink. Remove shrimp from pan; keep warm. Add celery and pepper to hot oil. Stir and fry until vegetables are cooked but retain some crispness. Add remaining vegetables, bouillon, seasonings, and shrimp. Mix and heat, stirring often. Mix cornstarch and water until free of lumps. Stir into hot mixture. Simmer, stirring constantly, until slightly thickened. Serve with heated chow mein noodles. Yield: About 6 servings.

Shrimp and Snow Peas

GOURMET INTERNATIONAL

See photo page 3

1 pound raw shrimp, shelled and deveined
2 tablespoons dry sherry
2 tablespoons cornstarch
1 teaspoon sugar
1 clove garlic, minced
3 tablespoons cooking oil
1/4 pound fresh mushrooms, thinly sliced
1 package (8 ounce) frozen snow peas, defrosted
2 chicken bouillon cubes
1 1/4 cups water
2 tablespoons soy sauce
1 can (5 ounce) water chestnuts, drained and
   sliced

Combine shrimp, sherry, 2 teaspoons cornstarch, sugar, and garlic; mix and let stand 10 minutes. Heat oil in Chinese wok or blazer pan of chafing dish over direct high flame. Add shrimp mixture, stir and fry until shrimp turns pink. Add mushrooms and cook until limp, stirring constantly. Add snow peas; stir and cook 1 minute. Combine remaining 4 teaspoons cornstarch, bouillon cubes, water, and soy sauce; mix well. Stir into hot shrimp mixture. Stir in water chestnuts. Cook, stirring until mixture thickens. Yield: About 4 servings.

Variations

Follow recipe for Shrimp and Snow Peas and change as suggested below.

BEEF AND SNOW PEAS: Substitute 1 pound beef sirloin, very thinly sliced and cut into strips 1/2 inch wide and 3 inches long, for shrimp. Stir and fry beef until it turns gray in color before adding snow peas. Substitute beef cubes for chicken bouillon cubes. Yield: 4 servings.

WIENERS AND SNOW PEAS: Substitute 1 pound fully cooked wieners for shrimp. Cut wieners diagonally into thirds. Stir and fry wieners in fat until heated before adding snow peas. Substitute beef cubes for chicken bouillon cubes. Yield: 4 servings.

Stir-fry (Chow) Broccoli or Carrots

GOURMET INTERNATIONAL

Prepare vegetables as suggested below. Cook as directed for asparagus (to left) except stir-fry vegetables just 1 minute, then add 1/2 cup chicken broth. Cover and lower flame to moderate. Cook until done but retain some crispness, 6 to 8 minutes, stirring occasionally.

BROCCOLI: Wash a 2-pound bunch of broccoli. Cut off flowerettes. Peel stems and cut into 1-inch diagonal slices. Yield: 6 servings.

CARROTS: Prepare 3 cups of diagonally sliced carrots. Wash and scrape or peel carrots. Cut into thin (1/8 to 1/4-inch) bias slices. Yield: 6 servings.

Chinese Pork and Green Beans

GOURMET INTERNATIONAL

3 tablespoons cooking oil
1 1/2 pounds boneless lean pork, cut into strips
   2 x 1/4 x 1/4 inches
1 medium large (2 1/2 to 3-inch) Spanish onion,
   thinly sliced
1 can (10 1/2 ounce) chicken broth
1 package (9 ounce) frozen cross cut green
   beans, defrosted
1/2 cup thinly sliced celery
1 can (5 ounce) water chestnuts, drained and
   sliced
1 can (4 ounce) sliced mushrooms, drained
3 tablespoons sherry, or water, as desired
3 tablespoons soy sauce
1 tablespoon cornstarch
1/2 teaspoon salt

Heat oil in Chinese wok or blazer pan of chafing dish, or in heavy fry pan on table top butane unit, over direct high flame. Sauté pork until well done over direct high flame, about 15 minutes, stirring often. Add onion slices; stir and cook until limp, 3 to 5 minutes. Add broth slowly; bring to a boil. Stir in beans, celery, water chestnuts, and mushrooms. Cover; cook until celery is tender yet retains a crispness, about 4 minutes. Combine remaining ingredients; mix until smooth and stir into hot mixture. Heat until mixture thickens, stirring constantly. Serve with hot Fluffy White Rice (page 46). Yield: 4 servings.

Sukiyaki

2 pounds sirloin steak or beef tenderloin
1/3 cup water
1/2 cup soy sauce
2 beef bouillon cubes
1 tablespoon sugar
3 tablespoons cooking oil
1 cup thinly sliced celery
6 green onions, cleaned and cut into 1-inch pieces
2 medium onions, cut in half and thinly sliced
1/2 pound fresh mushrooms, sliced
1 can (1 pound) bean sprouts, drained
2 cans (8 ounce) bamboo shoots, drained
1/2 pound spinach, washed and cut into narrow strips

Slice steak very thin (about 1/8-inch) across the grain and into 2 x 3-inch pieces. If meat is chilled in freezer until partially frozen it slices easier. Combine next 4 ingredients in measuring cup or small pitcher; set aside. Heat oil in Chinese wok on a ring or in blazer pan of chafing dish over direct high flame. Add celery and onions; cook until tender, but not brown, about 2 minutes, stirring constantly. Add mushrooms, bean sprouts, and bamboo shoots. Heat until vegetables are limp. Add spinach and meat. Cook, stirring constantly, until meat loses color and spinach is limp. Add soy mixture; cook and stir until mixture is hot and clear. Serve with hot Fluffy White Rice (page 46). Yield: About 6 servings.

INTRODUCTION CHAFING DISHES

TRADITIONAL CHAFING DISH: The traditional chafing dish (see photos pages 35, 42, 55 and 56) is the most popular of all tabletop cooking units. It includes a tray, stand or frame with built-in fuel container or lamp for fuel, flame adjuster and damper, water pan or jacket, sometimes called a bain marie, blazer pan and cover which fits into either the water pan or frame. Since both blazer and water pans are available the traditional chafing dish is really a combination double-boiler frying pan and the pans can be used singly or combined.

Chafing Dish Cooking

The chafing dish was a symbol of luxurious living and elegant eating in the gay 1890's. The handsome dish glowed in the candlelight while skillful chefs prepared fabulous creations for fascinated guests to enjoy at their leisure.

For many years lovely old silver, nickel, pewter and copper chafing dishes have been stored away with other family antiques. Now these treasures are being unburied and new ones purchased by busy young moderns who consider chafing dishes glamorous practical possessions.

Chafing dish cooking is a great fun way of cooking and serving food most practical for today's mode of living and entertaining.

Chafing dishes come in a wide variety of sizes, shapes and finishes. Small ones, just right for sauces and butters, two quart ones for small families and large ones that hold lots of food for lots of people. They come in copper, brass, silver, pewter, stainless steel and plain or color-coated aluminum. A design and finish for every taste.

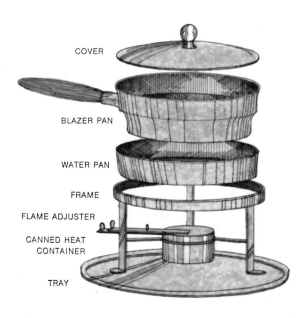

COVER

BLAZER PAN

WATER PAN

FRAME

FLAME ADJUSTER

CANNED HEAT CONTAINER

TRAY

ELECTRIC CHAFING DISH: The electric chafing dish offers complete flexibility in serving indoors or out, thermostatically controlled heat and cooking for two or a crowd. The guesswork has been eliminated when using an electric chafing dish for table top cook'n serve. Their only limitation is an electrical outlet. They like the traditional chafing dish can be used with or without the water pan. The instructions for care and use supplied by the manufacturer should be carefully read and followed.

Types of Chafing Dishes

The chafing dish family is a large one. There are the Traditional ones and the Specialty Pans designed to do a variety of culinary tricks easily and well. Master tabletop cooking in the traditional chafing dish and you'll want a number of the other attractive units.

SPECIALTY PANS: These pans used in conjunction with the stand and heating unit of your chafing dish or fondue make exciting table top cooking.

Round Crêpes or Omelet Pan — A heavy round pan 13 to 14 inches in diameter and 1 inch deep for use over direct heat (see photo page 38). Great for sautéeing meats, fish, chicken, fruits or frying eggs, pancakes, crêpes or blintzes.

Skillet — A heavy frying pan with sloping sides, 8 to 10 inches in diameter and 1¹/₂ to 2 inches deep very like the traditional chafing dish except that no water pan is included (see photo page 41). The skillet fits into a ring stand over direct heat and is excellent for the quick cooking of meats, chicken livers and foods usually prepared in the frying pan on top of the stove.

Crêpes Suzette Pan—Very like the skillet except the pan is only 1 to 1¹/₂ inches deep (see photo page 50). Great for frying pancakes, crêpes, etc.

Oval Omelet, Fish or Frying Pan — A heavy, shallow pan 11 to 13 inches long, 5 to 7 inches wide through center and 1 to 1¹/₂ inches deep for use over direct heat. Designed for omelets, heating rolled crêpes or blintzes, for scrambling eggs or frying brook or mountain trout or other small fish.

Fondue Pan, Pot or Caquelot — These are also in the chafing dish family. See pages 4 to 7.

Warmers — Heat-proof round or rectangular metal or ceramic containers on a stand over a single or double alcohol, canned heat, electric or candle warming unit (see photo page 45). Fine for keeping foods warm for buffet or patio service or to keep foods hot for tardy diners.

How to Use Chafing Dish

Get acquainted with the many parts of the chafing dish. Read the manufacturer's instructions and discover how easy it is to do plain and fancy cooking.

Select an easy-to-make food for your first table top cooking adventure. Think over each step before starting preparation and organize work to save a last minute crisis.

Before cooking remove cover, blazer and water pans from frame or stand. Place stand on metal or wooden tray to protect table top. Set fuel in place (see section on Chafing Dish Fuels below). If water pan is used set it in frame and add very hot water as needed to fill ¹/₄ full. Place blazer pan on water pan or over direct heat as recipe directs.

Do as much food preparation in advance as possible. The making of sauces, cleaning and chopping foods can generally be done ahead of time. Assemble cooking tools, foods and seasonings on a tray and place next to chafing dish. With planning chafing dish cooking is easy, uncomplicated, real fun.

Chafing Dish and Fondue Pot Fuels

Most chafing dishes use either canned heat or alcohol lamps for heat. Both electric and butane chafing dishes and heating units are available. Carefully follow care and use instructions provided by the manufacturers.

Keep an extra supply of fuel on hand so there will be no danger of running out in the middle of a party.

CANNED HEAT CHAFING DISHES: A holder is built into the chafing dish frame for the canned heat and a flame adjustor or damper is provided so heat can be controlled, opened wide for high heat, closed part way for low or closed completely to extinguish flame. Canned heat is safer than the alcohol type lamps.

Canned heat is available in hardware, paint, chain, department stores, drug stores and supermarkets. It comes in $2^5/8$ ounce cans which burn 50 to 60 minutes and 7 ounce cans which burn about 4 hours. The small size can is generally used for domestic units and the larger size for restaurant and institution units.

Remove lid from canned heat. Lower can into fuel container; cover with flame adjustor or damper.

ALCOHOL LAMP CHAFING DISHES: A holder is built into the chafing dish frame for the alcohol lamp. The lamp is partially filled with glass wool or a wick and has a cover or snuffer. The amount of heat produced from wick lamps is controlled with a screw which lengthens or shortens the wick for higher or lower flames. The lamps filled with glass wool have a flame adjustor which can be opened wide for high heat, half way for medium heat and closed for low heat. These units also have a flame snuffer used to extinguish the flame.

Denatured alcohol gives the hottest heat, has less odor and is not as expensive as rubbing or isopropyl alcohol. Denatured alcohol may be purchased at drug or hardware stores.

Never fill alcohol lamps more than $1/2$ full. To judge amount of alcohol needed allow about 1 tablespoonful of alcohol for each 12 minutes of cooking time. Fill lamp over sink or old newspapers as alcohol will ruin the finish on most furniture.

Wipe outside of lamp with dry cloth before lighting to catch any spillage. Cover lamp with flame snuffer and set in frame. Cover alcohol bottle.

Never refill lamp while burning or hot! Always extinguish wick lamp by turning wick low and covering with cap. Always extinguish glass wool type flame by closing flame adjustor and covering with flame snuffer. Cool lamp well after use, empty and dry before putting away.

To Flambé (Flame) Foods

Flaming food just before serving never fails to amaze and please. It's really a very simple trick, entirely safe if ordinary precautions are taken.

High-proof (high alcohol content) brandy, light or dark rum and cherry, orange or apricot liqueurs may all be used for flaming foods. Cointreau, Grand Marnier and kirsch are probably the favorite orange and cherry flavored liqueurs used for flaming.

Food being flamed must be hot and the liquor warmed for it to flame easily. To warm liquor pour the amount needed into a small long-handled pan or deep ladle and hold 3 to 4 inches above a very low heat to warm.

When flaming food stand back from chafing dish and pour warmed liquid over hot food. Tilt pan slightly and touch a long fireplace match to liquor vapor at edge of pan. Spoon flaming liquor over food until flame dies. Never add liquor, out of bottle or can, to food when flaming. The stream of liquor could catch fire with serious results. When flame is out all alcohol has burned away leaving only a delightfully distinctive lingering flavor.

To Clean Chafing Dishes

Let chafing dish cool, before cleaning, to prevent warping pans or discoloring outside finish.

Empty fuel container. See directions under Chafing Dish Fuels, above.

Remove handles and knobs before washing pans and cover, if possible. If handles and knob are not removable wash pans and cover without getting handles and knob into water.

Don't drop chafing dish parts into dishpan to soak. Permanent streaks and stains may form spoiling the finish.

APPETIZERS

Angels on Horseback See photo page 36

12 large oysters, well drained
1/2 teaspoon seasoned salt
Dash of pepper
12 small slices cooked chicken, 1/4-inch thick and size of oysters
6 thin slices bacon, cut in half crosswise
1 tablespoon butter or margarine
12 toast squares or rounds

Season oysters with salt and pepper; place each on a piece of chicken and wrap with bacon. Skewer with a wooden pick. Melt butter or margarine in blazer pan of chafing dish or attractive fry pan over butane unit over direct high flame. Cook until oysters and bacon are cooked, turning pieces as needed to cook evenly. Serve on hot toast squares or rounds. Yield: 12 bite-size appetizer portions; allow 3 portions per person.

Hot Dilly Shrimp

1 1/2 pounds raw shrimp, shelled, and deveined
3 tablespoons butter or margarine
3 tablespoons lemon juice
1 tablespoon finely chopped chives
3/4 teaspoon dill weed
1/2 teaspoon salt
Dash of pepper
1 teaspoon chopped parsley

Dry shrimp well on paper toweling. Melt butter or margarine in blazer pan of chafing dish or in fry pan on table-top butane unit over direct high flame. Add shrimp and heat until it cooks and turns pink, stirring often. Add next 5 ingredients; toss gently and heat. Sprinkle with parsley before serving. Place blazer pan in water jacket, if available, to keep warm while serving. Yield: 15 to 18 appetizer servings.

Hot Shrimp Tempter

See photo at right

1/4 cup butter or margarine
1/2 cup thinly sliced green onions
1/2 pound fresh mushrooms, washed and sliced
3 tablespoons flour
1 cup half and half (half milk, half cream)
1/4 cup Madeira wine or sherry, optional
1 teaspoon salt
1/8 teaspoon pepper
1 1/2 pounds cooked, shelled and deveined, fresh or defrosted frozen shrimp
2 tablespoons chopped parsley
Toast rounds

Heat butter or margarine in blazer pan of chafing dish over direct high flame. Add onions; cook, stirring constantly until limp. Add mushrooms, lower flame and cook until tender, about 5 minutes, stirring often. Sprinkle flour evenly over mushrooms; mix. Stir in half and half and wine, if desired; cook until thickened, stirring constantly. Season with salt, pepper. Fold in shrimp and heat, stirring often. Sprinkle chopped parsley over top. Place pan in water jacket for serving. Serve on buttered or plain toast rounds. Yield: About 12 appetizer servings.

HOT SHRIMP TEMPTER (PAGE 34)

Tiny Dolmadoes

Prepare a favorite well-seasoned meat ball mixture, or Swedish Meat Balls (page 46). Shape into rolls $3/4$-inch in diameter and $1^1/2$ inches long. Sauté rolls in butter or margarine in fry pan over moderate heat until cooked but not brown, 15 to 20 minutes, turning as needed. Brush rolls with catsup; wrap in fresh cabbage leaves which have been wilted in boiling salted water. Secure with wooden pick. Store covered in refrigerator until serving time. At serving time combine $3/4$ cup grape jelly, 1 cup catsup, $1/2$ teaspoon cinnamon, 3 or 4 whole cloves, and 2 tablespoons seedless raisins. Heat in blazer pan of chafing dish or in attractive fry pan over table-top butane unit. Stir often while heating. Turn flame to low, add cabbage rolls to sauce. Cover; heat, about 20 minutes. Serve on plates with small cocktail forks. Yield: About 24 servings.

WATER CHESTNUTS IN BACON (PAGE 37)

TINY DOLMADOES (ABOVE)

ANGELS ON HORSEBACK (PAGE 34)

Smoky Meat Balls

Follow recipe for Swedish Meat Balls (page 46). Shape meat ball mixture into small balls using 1 rounded teaspoonful for each ball. Brown and cook meat balls as directed in recipe but substitute 2 cups of favorite homemade or smoky commercial barbecue sauce for Medium Cream Sauce and omit caraway seed or dill weed. Stir 1/2 to 1 teaspoon liquid smoke into homemade sauce, if desired. Yield: About 36 meat balls.

Curried Meat Balls

Follow recipe for Smoky Meat Balls above and substitute Curry Sauce (page 48) for barbecue sauce. Yield: About 36 meat balls.

Appetizer Crêpes

Follow recipe for Feather-Light Pancakes (page 53); use 1 tablespoon batter for each pancake or crêpe. Spread each crêpe with a small amount of sour cream and caviar. Roll; secure with cocktail pick. Keep warm in lightly buttered blazer pan of chafing dish placed in water jacket. Yield: About 36 crêpes.

Fun-Do Appetizers Galore

See pages 8 to 14 for more fine 'n' fancy appetizers for every occasion.

Water Chestnuts in Bacon
See photo at left.

2 cans (5 ounce) water chestnuts (16 to 20), drained
1/2 cup French or Italian dressing
8 to 10 slices bacon, cut in half crosswise
1 tablespoon butter or margarine

Marinate water chestnuts in dressing 2 or 3 hours, stirring 2 or 3 times while marinating. Drain well. Wrap each water chestnut in a bacon slice. Secure with a wooden pick. Melt butter or margarine in blazer pan of chafing dish or attractive fry pan on butane unit over direct high flame. Cook until bacon is well browned, turning pieces as needed to cook evenly. Yield: About 16 to 20 bite-size appetizers.

Ham Bites in
Cherry Almond Sauce

2 tablespoons wine or cider vinegar
3 tablespoons water
1 teaspoon prepared mustard
1/4 teaspoon ground cloves
1 can (1 pound, 5 ounce) cherry pie filling
2 pounds fully cooked ham, cut into 3/4 inch cubes
1 tablespoon butter or margarine
1/3 cup toasted slivered almonds

Combine first 4 ingredients in blazer pan of chafing dish. Stir in cherry pie filling. Heat over direct moderate flame, stirring carefully, until bubbly hot. Reduce heat; add ham and butter or margarine and mix gently. Place blazer pan in water jacket; cover and heat to serving temperature. Just before serving sprinkle with almonds. Guests spear ham bites with long picks or cocktail forks. Yield: 20 to 30 appetizers.

Plain Omelet

8 eggs
¹/₄ cup milk or half and half (half milk, half cream)
1¹/₂ teaspoons salt
Dash pepper
2 tablespoons butter or margarine

Combine eggs, milk, salt, and pepper; beat slightly. Melt butter or margarine in omelet pan or blazer pan of chafing dish over direct high flame. Add egg mixture. Cook slowly until set, but still shiny. To speed cooking, run a spatula around edge of pan during cooking and lift omelet to let egg mixture flow below omelet. Fold omelet in half. Turn out of pan onto warm plate. Serve at once. Yield: 4 servings.

Omelet Variations

Follow recipe at left and change as suggested below:

STRAWBERRY OMELET (photo below): Omit pepper, ¹/₂ of the salt, and add 1 tablespoon sugar to egg mixture before cooking. Before folding omelet, spoon 1 cup sliced, sweetened strawberries over ¹/₂ of the omelet. Fold and sprinkle with confectioners' sugar. Yield: 4 servings.

FLAMING RUM OMELET: Omit pepper and ¹/₂ of the salt and add 1 tablespoon sugar to egg mixture before cooking. Fold omelet, sprinkle with confectioners' sugar. Drizzle ¹/₂ cup rum over omelet; ignite. Spoon flaming rum over omelet. Serve when flames die. Yield: 4 servings.

EGGS

CHEESE OMELET: Before folding omelet, sprinkle ³/₄ cup shredded Cheddar or American cheese and 1 teaspoon chopped chives over ¹/₂ of the omelet. Yield: 4 servings.

BACON, HAM, OR SAUSAGE OMELET: Before folding omelet, sprinkle ¹/₂ to ³/₄ cup crisp cooked bacon bits or hot diced fully cooked ham or sausage over ¹/₂ of the omelet. Yield: 4 servings.

JELLY OMELET: Before folding omelet, spread ¹/₂ cup softened jelly (or preserves) over ¹/₂ of the omelet. Yield: 4 servings.

Scrambled Eggs

3 tablespoons butter or margarine
8 eggs
¹/₂ cup milk, or half and half (half milk, half cream)
1¹/₂ teaspoons salt
Dash pepper

Melt butter or margarine in blazer pan of chafing dish over direct high flame or in heavy fry pan on table top butane unit. Combine remaining ingredients; beat slightly. Pour egg mixture into pan. Cook to desired consistency, stirring often. Set blazer pan in water jacket, if available, or turn flame low to keep warm while serving. Yield: 4 to 6 servings.

Variations

Follow recipe for Scrambled Eggs (at left) and make changes as suggested below:

ITALIAN EGGS: Brown 2 tablespoons finely chopped onion in butter or margarine over direct high flame. Add 1 medium tomato, diced, and ³/₄ teaspoon oregano; heat. Reduce milk to ¹/₄ cup and add egg mixture to tomatoes. Just before serving, sprinkle ¹/₂ to ³/₄ cup shredded Mozzarella or Cheddar cheese and 1 teaspoon minced parsley over top. Cover pan and allow cheese to soften. Yield: 4 to 6 servings.

MEXICANA EGGS: Sauté ¹/₄ cup chopped green pepper and 2 tablespoons sliced green onions in butter or margarine before adding egg mixture. Fold ¹/₂ cup crisp cooked bacon pieces, ¹/₂ cup chopped fresh tomatoes, ¹/₄ cup sliced pitted ripe or stuffed olives, and ¹/₂ teaspoon chili powder into eggs just before they set. Yield: 4 to 6 servings.

BACON OR HAM EGGS: Stir ¹/₃ to 1 cup crisp cooked bacon pieces or finely chopped fully cooked ham or Canadian bacon into egg mixture before cooking. Yield: 4 to 6 servings.

HERB EGGS WITH SOUR CREAM: Add a pinch or two of basil, chives, rosemary, or fines herbes, as desired, to egg mixture before cooking. Fold ¹/₄ cup dairy sour cream into eggs as they start to set. Yield: 4 to 6 servings.

ENTRÉES

Beef Stroganoff

2 pounds sirloin steak, sliced $1/4$-inch thick
$1/2$ cup butter or margarine
2 cups coarsely chopped onion
2 cloves garlic, minced, optional
$1/2$ pound fresh mushrooms, sliced
2 tablespoons flour
$1/2$ teaspoon salt
Dash of pepper
1 can ($10^1/2$ ounce) beef bouillon
$1/4$ cup dry white wine, optional
$1/2$ pint (1 cup) dairy sour cream
1 teaspoon Worcestershire sauce
Chopped parsley or fresh dill

Chill steak in freezer until partially frozen to make slicing easier. Cut steak into strips 2 x $1/4$ x $1/4$ inches. Heat $1/4$ cup butter or margarine in blazer pan of chafing dish or in fry pan on table top butane unit, over direct high flame. Brown meat well; remove from pan and keep hot. Add remaining butter or margarine, onion and garlic; cook until onion is tender, stirring often. Add mushrooms; cook until tender. Stir in flour, salt, and pepper. Add bouillon; cook until thickened, stirring constantly. Reduce flame to medium low; stir in wine, if used, sour cream, and Worcestershire sauce. Add meat; mix carefully. Cover and heat. Sprinkle with parsley or dill. Serve on hot buttered rice or noodles. Yield: About 6 to 8 servings.

Noodles Romanoff

$1/4$ cup butter or margarine
2 tablespoons finely chopped onion
1 small clove garlic, finely minced
$1/2$ pint (1 cup) creamed cottage cheese
$1/2$ pint (1 cup) dairy sour cream
$1/2$ teaspoon salt
$1/2$ pound egg noodles, cooked, drained and seasoned

Melt butter or margarine in blazer pan of chafing dish over direct high flame. Add onion and garlic; cook until tender, stirring constantly. Reduce heat. Stir in cheese, sour cream, and salt; mix. Add noodles; toss lightly to coat well. Heat. Sprinkle with parsley. Yield: About 4 servings.

Flaming Polynesian Ham with Curried Rice

See photo at right

$1/4$ cup sugar
$1/4$ cup cornstarch
$1/4$ teaspoon salt
1 cup pineapple juice
$1/3$ cup orange marmalade
$1/3$ cup vinegar or lemon juice
1 pound fully cooked ham, cut into 1-inch cubes
1 can (11 ounce) mandarin orange sections, drained
1 can ($13^1/2$ ounce) pineapple tidbits, undrained
$3/4$ cup seedless green grapes, cantaloupe or honeydew melon chunks
$1/2$ cup Cointreau, optional
6 cups Fluffy White or Curried Rice (page 46)
$1/2$ cup toasted silvered almonds, optional

Combine first 3 ingredients in blazer pan of chafing dish or heavy fry pan on table top butane unit; mix well. Place over direct high flame; stir in pineapple juice, marmalade, vinegar, or lemon juice, cook, stirring constantly until thickened. Reduce flame to low and fold in ham; heat. Add fruits and $1/4$ cup Cointreau, if used. Heat. Place blazer pan in water jacket, if available. Pour remaining Cointreau over mixture; ignite. When flame dies, serve atop hot rice; sprinkle with almonds. Yield: About 6 servings.

Sweet and Sour Pork or Chicken

Follow recipe for Flaming Polynesian Ham with Curried Rice above and substitute 2 to $2^1/2$ cups diced cooked pork or chicken for ham and omit Cointreau. Yield: About 6 servings.

Oceania Franks or Wieners on Rice

Follow recipe for Flaming Polynesian Ham with Curried Rice above and substitute 1 pound fully cooked franks or wieners, cut in thirds, for ham. Flame, if desired. Yield: About 6 servings.

FLAMING POLYNESIAN HAM (PAGE 40)

SHRIMP CURRY (PAGE 43)

Indian Lamb Curry

2 tablespoons butter or margarine
1¼ cups chopped onion
1 small clove garlic, minced
2 tablespoons flour
2 teaspoons brown sugar
2 teaspoons curry powder, or to taste
1 teaspoon salt
¼ teaspoon ginger
⅛ teaspoon pepper
1¼ cups chopped peeled apple
1 can (8 ounce) tomato sauce
1½ cups water
2 chicken or beef bouillon cubes
3 cups diced cooked lamb
½ cup flaked coconut, optional

Melt butter or margarine in blazer pan of chafing dish over direct high flame. Add onion and garlic; cook onion until tender, stirring often. Stir in next 6 ingredients. Add apple, tomato sauce, water, and bouillon cubes; mix. Reduce heat; cover and simmer gently, about 30 minutes. Add lamb; cover and heat. Sprinkle coconut over top. Serve with hot Fluffy White Rice (page 46). Yield: 6 servings.

Crab Newburg

Prepare Cream Sauce (Medium) (page 48). Cook 2 tablespoons minced onion in butter or margarine before stirring in flour. Mix 2 tablespoons dry white wine or sherry, optional, 1 teaspoon lemon juice, ¼ teaspoon grated lemon rind, and 2 beaten egg yolks. Add to sauce slowly, stirring constantly. Fold in 1 package (12 ounce) frozen crab meat, defrosted and flaked. Mix gently; cover and heat. Serve on hot toast points, toasted cornbread squares, or patty shells. Yield: About 4 to 6 servings.

Lobster Newburg

Follow recipe for Crab Newburg above and substitute 2 cans (5 or 6 ounce) lobster, flaked, for crab meat. Yield: About 4 to 6 servings.

Chicken or Turkey Newburg

Follow recipe for Crab Newburg above and substitute 1 can (4 ounce) sliced mushrooms, drained, for onion. Omit lemon juice and rind. Substitute 1½ cups cooked diced chicken or turkey for crab meat. Serve on hot toast, corn bread or patty shells. Yield: About 4 to 6 servings.

Chicken à la Russe

⅓ cup flour
2 teaspoons salt
⅛ teaspoon white pepper
¼ teaspoon garlic salt
3 chicken breasts, cut in half
⅓ cup butter or margarine
½ teaspoon each, rosemary and thyme
¼ pound fresh mushrooms, sliced, about 1½ cups
1 cup (½ pint) dairy sour cream
1½ tablespoons chopped chives
1 tablespoon chopped parsley

Mix first 4 ingredients; dredge chicken pieces in flour mixture. Melt butter or margarine in blazer pan of chafing dish or in heavy fry pan over table top butane unit over direct moderate flame. Brown chicken evenly, turning as needed. Sprinkle herbs over chicken. Cover; cook over low direct flame until tender, turning occasionally, 30 to 40 minutes. Remove cover and crisp chicken; remove pieces from pan and keep warm. Add mushrooms. Cook until tender; stir in sour cream and chives. Heat, stirring gently. Return chicken pieces to pan; cover and heat. Before serving sprinkle with parsley and place blazer pan in water jacket. Yield: 4 to 6 servings.

Curry Variations

Follow recipe for Indian Lamb Curry and change as follows.

CHICKEN CURRY, MADRAS STYLE: Substitute 3 cups diced cooked chicken for lamb.

SHRIMP CURRY, MADRAS STYLE: See photo at left. Substitute 1 pound cooked, cleaned, and deveined shrimp for lamb.

Turkey, Chicken, or Ham à la King

Prepare Cream Sauce (Medium) using light cream or half and half (half milk, half cream) page 48.

Fold in 1 to 1¼ cups cooked diced turkey, chicken, or fully cooked ham, ½ cup cooked diced celery, ¼ cup cooked, diced green pepper, 1 can (4 ounce) sliced mushrooms, drained, 2 tablespoons diced pimientoes, and 1 well beaten egg yolk. Stir in 2 tablespoons sherry, if desired. Serve at once on hot biscuits, toast, or patty shells. Sprinkle with toasted slivered almonds. Yield: About 4 cups, 6 servings.

Chicken in Wine—Coq au Vin

3 tablespoons flour
1 teaspoon salt
¹/₂ teaspoon paprika
¹/₈ teaspoon nutmeg
1 3-pound frying chicken, cut into serving
 pieces
4 slices bacon, cut in 1-inch pieces
¹/₄ cup butter or margarine
1 cup sliced fresh mushrooms
12 small (1-inch) onions, halved
1 clove garlic, minced
¹/₄ teaspoon leaf thyme
¹/₄ teaspoon marjoram
1 small bay leaf
¹/₄ cup brandy or cognac, optional
1 cup dry red wine (Burgundy or Beaujolais)
Chopped parsley

Mix first 4 ingredients; dredge chicken in flour mixture. Fry bacon pieces until crisp in blazer pan of chafing dish or in heavy fry pan on table top butane unit over direct high flame. Remove bacon pieces from pan; drain and save. Add butter or margarine. Brown chicken in fat, turning pieces as needed to brown evenly. Sprinkle any remaining flour over top. Add mushrooms, onions, garlic, and herbs; cook over moderate direct flame until mushrooms are tender. If desired, pour brandy or cognac over chicken; ignite. When flame dies; mix gently and pour wine over top. Cover and cook over low flame until chicken is fork tender, about 1 hour. Just before serving sprinkle with parsley. Yield: 4 to 6 servings.

Sloppy Joe Burgers

2 tablespoons butter or margarine
1 cup chopped onion
1 pound ground beef
1 teaspoon salt
¹/₂ teaspoon chili powder
1 tablespoon flour
¹/₂ cup catsup
¹/₂ cup water
1 teaspoon Worcestershire sauce

Melt butter or margarine in blazer pan of chafing dish over direct high flame. Add onion and meat; cook until meat is gray, stirring frequently. Add remaining ingredients; mix, cover, and cook until meat and onions are tender, about 30 minutes. Serve on hot toasted buns. Yield: 4 to 6 servings.

Hot German-Style Potato Salad

¹/₄ pound bacon, diced
³/₄ cup thinly sliced celery
¹/₂ cup sliced green or chopped onion
1¹/₂ tablespoons flour
³/₄ cup water
¹/₃ cup vinegar
2 tablespoons sugar
1¹/₂ teaspoons salt
1 teaspoon prepared mustard
¹/₄ teaspoon celery seed
Dash of pepper
4 cups sliced cooked potatoes
2 tablespoons finely chopped parsley

Brown bacon in blazer pan of chafing dish over direct high flame. Remove bacon from drippings, drain and save. Add celery and onion to drippings; cook until onion is limp. Stir in next 8 ingredients. Cook until thickened, stirring constantly. Fold in potatoes, parsley, and bacon. Cover and heat. Place blazer pan in water jacket to keep food hot while serving. Yield: 6 servings.

In-a-Hurry Creamed Dried Beef

Prepare In-a-Hurry Cream Sauce (page 48). Stir in 1¹/₂ teaspoons prepared mustard, 1 teaspoon instant minced onion, or 1 tablespoon thinly sliced green onion, if desired. Fold in 1 jar (4 or 5 ounce) sliced dried beef, torn into small pieces; heat. Serve on hot buttered toast or toasted English muffins. Yield: 3 to 4 servings.

Quick Sausage Noodle Supper

1 can (10¹/₂ ounce) condensed tomato soup
¹/₂ cup milk
¹/₂ cup cooked diced celery
¹/₃ cup cooked diced onion
6 fully-cooked smoked pork or garlic sausage
 links, cut into ¹/₂ inch slices
3 cups hot cooked buttered and seasoned
 noodles

Combine ingredients, except noodles, in metal fondue pot; mix. Cover; place over moderate direct flame and heat to serving temperature. To serve, spoon over hot noodles. Yield: About 6 servings.

Hot Potato Salad With Franks

See photo below

Fold 1 pound of fully cooked frankfurters or wieners, cut crosswise into 1-inch slices, into Hot German-Style Potato Salad (recipe at left) at the time the potatoes are added. Yield: 6 servings.

Quick Patio Beans

2 cans (1 pound 5 ounce) pork and beans with
   tomato sauce
1/3 cup chili sauce
1/4 cup thinly sliced green onion
1/4 cup well drained sweet pickle or India relish
1 tablespoon molasses or brown sugar
1/2 teaspoon prepared mustard
2 dashes hot pepper sauce, optional

Combine ingredients in blazer pan of chafing dish or fondue pot. Place over moderate direct flame; cover and heat to serving temperature, 15 to 20 minutes. Stir often. Yield: About 6 servings.

BACON 'N' BEANS (see photo below): Prepare Patio Beans (recipe above); sprinkle 1/3 to 1/2 cup hot crisp bacon bits over beans just before serving. Yield: 6 servings.

Swedish Meat Balls

1 pound ground beef
1 cup fine fresh bread crumbs
1/4 cup finely chopped onion
1/2 cup milk
1 egg
1 teaspoon salt
1/8 teaspoon nutmeg
1/8 teaspoon pepper
1/4 cup butter or margarine
Cream Sauce (Medium) (page 48)
1/2 teaspoon caraway seed or dill weed

Combine first 8 ingredients. Mix well and shape into balls using 1 tablespoonful for each ball. Melt butter or margarine in blazer pan of chafing dish or fry pan on table top butane unit over direct high flame. Brown meat balls well, turning as needed to brown evenly. Cover; turn flame to low. Cook just until done, 15 or 20 minutes. Tip pan slightly and spoon off any excess fat. Combine hot Cream Sauce and caraway seed or dill weed. Pour over meat balls; stir gently. Place over water jacket, if available, for serving. Serve with hot buttered noodles, if desired. Yield: About 16 meat balls, 4 servings.

Curried Fish or Seafood

Prepare Curry Sauce (page 48) in blazer pan of chafing dish over direct low flame. Stir in 1 teaspoon lemon juice and 1/4 teaspoon grated lemon rind. Fold in 1 to 1 1/2 cups diced fish or boned and flaked or diced seafood (salmon, tuna, halibut, shrimp, crab meat, or lobster) and 1 can (3 ounce) sliced mushrooms, drained, and 1 tablespoon diced pimientoes. Serve on hot rice, biscuits, or patty shells. Yield: About 3 1/2 to 4 cups, 6 servings.

Fettuccini

1/2 cup soft butter or margarine
1/2 cup whipping cream or half and half (half milk, half cream)
1 pound medium egg noodles, cooked, drained, and seasoned
1 cup shredded Parmesan cheese
Ground pepper
Ground nutmeg

Melt butter or margarine in blazer pan of chafing dish over direct high flame. Stir in cream or half and half; heat until bubbly to center of pan. Add noodles; sprinkle with cheese and toss lightly. Sprinkle with pepper and nutmeg. Yield: 6 servings.

RICE AND PASTA

Fluffy White Rice

Cook favorite quick cook (precooked long-grain) rice in blazer pan of chafing dish over direct moderate flame. Use ingredients and method for cooking, suggested on package, for 4 or 6 servings. Fluff rice with fork before serving. Insert blazer pan in water jacket to keep rice hot for serving.

Variations

Follow recipe for Fluffy White Rice; change as suggested below.

ALMOND RICE: Stir 2 tablespoons butter or margarine and 1/2 cup toasted slivered almonds into Fluffy White Rice. Excellent with poultry, seafood, and meat entrées.

CURRIED RICE: Stir in 1/2 teaspoon curry powder (or to taste), 1/2 cup diced cooked celery and 1/2 cup toasted slivered almonds, if desired, into Fluffy White Rice. Delicious with pork, chicken or seafood dishes.

ORANGE RICE: Substitute 1 cup orange juice for 1 cup water. Add 1 to 1 1/2 tablespoons grated orange rind and a pinch of thyme, if desired, to liquids. A treat with ham, duck, or pork.

PARSLEY WHITE RICE: Stir in 2 tablespoons butter or margarine and 2 to 3 tablespoons chopped parsley. Serve with favorite meat, fish, or poultry entrée.

PILAF: Melt 2 tablespoons butter or margarine in blazer pan of chafing dish over direct high flame. Add 1/3 cup chopped onion and 1/2 cup sliced celery; sauté until onion is tender. Add 2 beef bouillon cubes to water; prepare same as Fluffy White Rice and omit salt. Just right for serving with lamb kabobs, meat balls, steaks, etc.

FRUITED NUT RICE: Cook 1/3 cup light raisins with rice. Stir 1/2 teaspoon sugar, 1/2 teaspoon grated orange rind, and 1/2 cup coarsely chopped pecans into Fluffy White Rice. Excellent with pork, chicken, duck, or ham.

Most of these sauces can only be made in units with adjustable heat controls.

What Sauces To Serve?

SAUCE	Page	BEEF	LAMB	PORK, HAM CANADIAN BACON	SAU-SAGES	FISH and SEAFOOD	POULTRY CHICKEN TURKEY
CREAM SAUCE—CURRY	48	✔	✔	✔	✔	✔	✔
CREAM SAUCE—HORSERADISH	48	✔		✔	✔	✔	
CREAM SAUCE—MORNAY	48	✔		✔	✔	✔	
BARBECUE	49	✔	✔	✔	✔	✔	
BEARNAISE	49	✔			✔	✔	
SWEET & SOUR TOMATO	48	✔		✔	✔	✔	✔
SOUR CREAM—MUSTARD	47	✔	✔	✔	✔	✔	
SOUR CREAM—MUSTARD RELISH	47	✔	✔	✔	✔	✔	
SOUR CREAM—BLUE CHEESE	47	✔					
REMOULADE	49					✔	
HERB BUTTER FOR DIPPING	47	✔	✔	✔	✔	✔	
SPICY SAUCE	48	✔			✔	✔	
ANCHOVY BUTTER	47	✔				✔	
GARLIC BUTTER	47	✔	✔		✔	✔	✔

Herb Butter Dipping Sauce For Beef Fondue

1 cup butter or margarine, melted
2 tablespoons lemon juice
1/4 teaspoon fines herbes blend
Dash of hot pepper sauce

Combine ingredients; mix. Yield: About 1 cup.

Variations

Follow recipe for Herb Butter Dipping Sauce (above) and change as suggested below.

ANCHOVY BUTTER SAUCE: Omit fines herbes blend. Add 2 to 4 anchovy fillets which have been finely chopped.

GARLIC BUTTER SAUCE: Omit fines herbes blend. Add 1 clove garlic, quartered, and 1 tablespoon finely chopped chives. Let stand 15 to 20 minutes then remove garlic.

Sour Cream Mustard Sauce

1/2 pint (1 cup) dairy sour cream
1/2 cup salad dressing
1/4 cup prepared mustard
1 tablespoon finely chopped onion
Dash of hot pepper sauce, optional

Combine ingredients; mix well. Serve cold. Delicious with beef, fish, ham or hot dogs. Yield: About 1 3/4 cups.

Variations

Follow recipe for Sour Cream Mustard Sauce (above) and change as suggested below:

MUSTARD RELISH SAUCE: Fold in 1/4 cup drained sweet pickle relish. Yield: About 2 cups.

BLUE CHEESE SAUCE: Omit mustard and onion and fold in 1/3 cup crumbled blue cheese and 1/4 teaspoon Worcestershire sauce. Yield: About 1 3/4 cups.

Cream Sauce (Medium)*

1/4 cup butter or margarine
3 to 4 tablespoons flour
1/2 teaspoon salt
Dash of pepper
2 cups milk, light cream or half and half (half milk, half cream)

Melt butter or margarine in blazer pan of chafing dish or metal fondue pot over direct low flame. Stir in flour and seasonings. Stir in milk slowly and cook, stirring constantly, until thick and smooth. Yield: About 2 1/4 cups.

*Use for making à la king and creamed entrées or vegetables. For a thin cream sauce reduce butter or margarine and flour to 2 tablespoons. Use as a soup base.

Sauce Variations

Follow recipe for Cream Sauce (Medium) and change as follows.

CHEESE SAUCE: Add 1 to 2 cups shredded process or natural American or Swiss cheese and 1/2 teaspoon prepared mustard to sauce; stir until cheese melts. Fine for serving with meat loaf, burgers, ham, fish, or seafood or for making au gratin dishes. Yield: About 2 3/4 cups.

EGG SAUCE: Fold 2 to 4 coarsely chopped or thinly sliced hard cooked eggs and 1 teaspoon prepared mustard into sauce. Delicious on toast or waffles or as a sauce with meat loaf or fish. Yield: About 2 1/2 cups.

MORNAY SAUCE: Add 1/3 cup each of grated or shredded Swiss and American or Parmesan cheese into sauce. Stir until cheese melts. Excellent with fish. Yield: About 2 1/2 cups.

CURRY SAUCE: Blend 2 to 3 teaspoons curry powder, 1 teaspoon sugar, 1/8 teaspoon ginger, and 1/4 cup minced onion into butter or margarine when preparing sauce. Cook, stirring constantly, until onion is tender before adding flour. Excellent for making chicken, lamb, or seafood curries. Yield: About 2 1/3 cups.

HORSERADISH SAUCE: Prepare 1/2 recipe of sauce and fold in 3 tablespoons horseradish and 1 cup sour or whipped cream just before serving. Delicious with beef, corned beef, or ham. Yield: About 2 1/4 cups.

In-A-Hurry Cream Sauce (Medium)

Stir 1/2 cup milk or half and half (half milk, half cream) into 1 can (10 1/2 ounce) condensed cream of celery soup. Heat to serving temperature in blazer pan of chafing dish or metal fondue pot over direct moderate flame, stirring constantly. Yield: About 2 cups.

IN-A-HURRY CHEESE SAUCE: Prepare as for In-a-Hurry Cream Sauce (Medium) but substitute 1 can (10 3/4 ounce) condensed cheddar cheese soup for celery.

Sweet and Sour Tomato Sauce

1 jar (12 ounces) pineapple or apricot
    preserves or thick orange marmalade
1/3 cup catsup
3 tablespoons lemon juice
2 tablespoons brown sugar
1 tablespoon soy sauce
1/4 teaspoon ginger

Combine ingredients in blazer pan of chafing dish or fondue pot; mix well. Place over medium direct heat; simmer gently until thickened, about 10 minutes; stir occasionally. Serve warm. Delicious on ham or beef balls, ham squares, beef bites, hot dog chunks or cocktail wieners. Yield: About 1 1/4 cups.

Spicy Sauce

1 cup catsup
2 tablespoons vinegar
3/4 teaspoon prepared horseradish
Dash of hot pepper sauce

Combine ingredients; blend well. Serve cold. Yield: About 1 cup.

BEARNAISE SAUCE

Remoulade Sauce

1 cup salad dressing or mayonnaise
3 tablespoons well drained sweet pickle relish
1 tablespoon finely chopped green onion
1 tablespoon chopped capers
1 tablespoon minced parsley
1 tablespoon vinegar
1 teaspoon prepared mustard

Combine ingredients; mix and chill. Yield: About 1¼ cups.

Barbecue Sauce

1 cup catsup or chili sauce
¾ cup water
¼ cup vinegar or lemon juice
3 tablespoons sugar
2 teaspoons Worcestershire sauce
2 teaspoons chili powder, or to taste
¼ teaspoon salt
⅓ cup finely chopped onion
⅓ cup finely chopped celery, optional
¼ to ½ teaspoon liquid smoke, optional

Combine ingredients in blazer pan of chafing dish or fondue pot; mix. Place over medium direct flame; heat to simmering stage, stirring often. Lower heat; cover and simmer gently 10 to 15 minutes. Yield: About 2½ cups.

Bearnaise Sauce

GOURMET INTERNATIONAL

See photo at left

½ cup butter or margarine
¼ cup water or dry white wine
3 tablespoons tarragon or cider vinegar
2 teaspoons finely chopped onions or shallots
¼ teaspoon salt
Dash of pepper
3 egg yolks
½ cup mayonnaise or salad dressing

Combine first 7 ingredients in container of an electric blender, if available. Whiz until ingredients are finely chopped. If no blender is available beat with wire whisk or beater until light and fluffy. Pour into blazer pan of small chafing dish or metal fondue pot over direct low flame. Cook, stirring until mixture thickens. Remove from heat and stir in mayonnaise or salad dressing. Serve with meat, fish, or seafood fondue dishes or with favorite steaks or burgers. Yield: About 1½ cups.

FLAMING STRAWBERRY CRÊPES (PAGE 51)

CRÊPES, PANCAKES AND BLINTZES

Call them crêpes, pancakes, hot cakes, or blintzes. Whether plain or fancy they're great eating any meal of the day. Try any one of the following; prepare them in the crêpes suzette or blazer pan of chafing dish over direct high flame right at the table, or prepare them ahead of time; dust cakes with confectioners' sugar, roll and wrap separately in plastic film or waxed paper, and refrigerate until serving time. To reheat; unwrap, unroll, fill, and heat in lightly buttered blazer or crêpes suzette pan over direct high flame. Serve with a piping hot sauce or syrup made in the fondue pot. See pages 21, 23 and 24.

Crêpes Suzette

GOURMET INTERNATIONAL ™

Recipe Feather-Light pancakes (page 53)
1/4 cup butter or margarine
3 tablespoons sugar
1/2 cup orange juice
2 teaspoons lemon juice
1/3 cup orange liqueur (Grand Marnier or Cointreau)
1 tablespoon grated orange rind
1/2 teaspoon grated lemon rind
1/2 cup toasted slivered almonds

Prepare pancakes using 2 or 3 tablespoons batter. Melt butter or margarine in blazer pan of chafing dish or crêpes suzette pan over table top burner or butane unit over direct high flame. Stir in sugar, juices, 3 tablespoons liqueur, and rinds. Heat until bubbly, stirring constantly. Roll up pancakes; place in sauce and heat. Turn crêpes carefully to heat evenly. Spoon sauce over crêpes while heating. Drizzle remaining liqueur over crêpes; ignite. Let flame die down, sprinkle with almonds and serve. Note: The 16 pancakes may be made ahead of time and refrigerated until serving time. See directions in introduction (above). Yield: 16 crêpes.

Flaming Strawberry Crêpes

GOURMET INTERNATIONAL ™

See photo at left

Prepare Crêpes with Sour Cream and Strawberries (recipe follows). Just before serving, drizzle 1/4 cup orange liqueur (Cointreau or Grand Marnier) over crêpes; ignite. Serve when flame dies down. Yield: 16 crêpes.

Crêpes with Sour Cream and Strawberries

GOURMET INTERNATIONAL ™

16 Feather-Light Pancakes (page 53)
1 pint (2 cups) dairy sour cream
3 tablespoons sugar
2 tablespoons orange liqueur (Cointreau or Grand Marnier), optional
2 cups sweetened sliced strawberries
2 tablespoons butter or margarine
Confectioners' sugar

Prepare pancakes as directed for Crêpes Suzette (at left) ahead of serving time. Combine sour cream, sugar, and orange liqueur, if desired. Spread pancakes with an equal amount of sour cream mixture and a few sliced berries; roll up. Arrange rolls in shallow casserole; cover and store in refrigerator until serving time. To heat melt butter or margarine in crêpes suzette or blazer pan of chafing dish over direct high flame. Heat pancake rolls, turning carefully to heat evenly. Add remaining strawberries; heat. Sprinkle with confectioners' sugar. Yield: 16 crêpes.

Cheese Blintzes

See photo below

GOURMET INTERNATIONAL ™

1 recipe Feather-Light Pancakes (page 53)
1 cup small curd creamed cottage cheese
1 package (3 ounce) cream cheese, room tem-
    perature
¼ cup sugar
1 teaspoon vanilla
½ teaspoon grated lemon or orange rind
2 tablespoons butter or margarine
Sour cream
Fruit sauce (page 21) or preserves (strawberry,
    blueberries, or cherry)

Prepare pancakes ahead of serving time, using 2 or 3 tablespoons batter and a 6- or 7-inch pan. Cook cakes, browning one side only. Blend cheeses, sugar, vanilla, and lemon or orange rind. Spoon an equal amount of filling across center of cooked side of cakes. Fold 2 opposite edges of pancake over filling and roll up pancake to make blintzes. Cool; arrange in shallow casserole or dish. Cover and refrigerate until serving time. To heat at serving time melt butter or margarine in blazer pan of chafing dish over direct high flame. Lightly brown blintzes, turning to brown evenly. Serve hot with sour cream and fruit sauce or preserves (strawberry, cherry, or blueberry). Yield: 12 blintzes.

Fun-Do Pancake Syrups

Great syrups and sauces, just right for serving with pancakes, crêpes, and waffles may be found on pages 21, 23, and 24.

Feather-Light Pancakes

1 cup sifted flour
2 tablespoons sugar
1¹/₂ teaspoons baking powder
¹/₂ teaspoon salt
2 eggs, beaten slightly
1¹/₄ cups milk
3 tablespoons melted shortening or cooking oil

Combine first 4 ingredients; sift into mixing bowl. Combine eggs, milk, and shortening or oil; stir into dry ingredients. Mix just until dry ingredients are moistened. Pour ¹/₄ cup batter, for each pancake, into hot, well greased crêpes suzette pan or blazer pan of chafing dish over direct high flame. Cook until top is full of bubbles, edges dry and underside browned; turn and brown second side. When pancakes are being prepared for crêpes they may be cooked ahead of time, as desired, sprinkled with confectioners' sugar, rolled and wrapped singly in waxed paper or plastic film and stored in refrigerator for reheating at time of serving. Yield: About 8 4-inch pancakes, 16 crêpes or 12 blintzes.

Variations

Follow recipe for Feather-Light Pancakes and change as follows.

APPLE PANCAKES: Fold in ²/₃ cup finely chopped peeled apple. Serve with Hot Spiced Honey Butter (page 24). Yield: About 10 to 12 4-inch pancakes.

DESSERT PANCAKES: Increase eggs to 3, and milk to 1¹/₂ cups, and stir in 1 teaspoon grated orange rind. Yield: About 10 4-inch pancakes.

PECAN PANCAKES: Fold in ¹/₂ to ³/₄ cup coarsely chopped pecans. Serve with syrup or Peach Sauce (page 21). Yield: About 10 to 12 4-inch pancakes.

PINEAPPLE PANCAKES: Fold in ¹/₂ cup well drained canned crushed pineapple and ¹/₂ teaspoon grated orange rind. Serve with syrup or sour cream or soft ice cream with cherry or strawberry preserves. Yield: About 10 4-inch pancakes.

SOUR CREAM PANCAKES: Increase sugar to 3 tablespoons, add a dash of nutmeg and substitute ¹/₃ cup dairy sour cream and ³/₄ cup half and half (half milk, half cream) for sweet milk. Yield: About 8 4-inch pancakes.

In-A-Hurry Pancakes

1 cup prepared pancake mix
1 tablespoon sugar
1 or 2 eggs
1 cup milk
3 tablespoons cooking oil or melted shortening

Combine pancake mix and sugar in mixing bowl. Stir in remaining ingredients. Bake as directed for Feather-Light Pancakes at left. Yield: About 8 4-inch pancakes.

S'More Pancake Favorites

JAM-FILLED PANCAKES: Spread favorite pancakes with thick strawberry or raspberry preserves or orange marmalade; roll. Sprinkle with confectioners' sugar and serve at once.

PANCAKE WEDGES: Spread favorite pancakes with jelly, hot mincemeat, or peanut butter and jelly; fold pancake in half or quarters. Sprinkle with confectioners' sugar and serve at once.

DINNER PANCAKES: Prepare Feather-Light or In-a-Hurry Pancakes above. Spread with favorite creamed entrée (chicken à la king, creamed seafood, or fish, ham à la king, etc.); roll. Serve hot with additional creamed mixture.

DESSERTS

Preparing easy and elegant chafing dish desserts, with a bit of a flair right at the table, will amaze, delight, and please family and friends. Try one or two of the following easy recipes and you'll think of many more to try.

Fun-Do Dessert Fondues

Are great crowd pleasers. See recipes for dessert fondues on pages 16-21.

Strawberries Flambé

GOURMET INTERNATIONAL ™

See photo page 3.

2 tablespoons butter or margarine
1/4 cup sugar
1/4 cup orange juice
2 teaspoons grated orange rind
1/4 cup brandy, kirsch or Cointreau
1 quart fresh strawberries, washed, stemmed, and dried
Strawberry, vanilla, New York, or rum ice cream or pound cake slices

Melt butter or margarine in blazer pan of chafing dish over direct high flame. Stir in sugar, juice, rind, and 2 tablespoons brandy, kirsch, or Cointreau; cook until mixture is full of bubbles. Fold in strawberries; heat about 1 minute. Warm remaining liqueur in ladle; pour over strawberries and ignite. When flame dies, spoon over ice cream or cake. Yield: About 3³/₄ cups sauce.

Dessert Crêpes, Pancakes, and Blintzes

Are always dessert winners. See the easy-to-follow recipes on pages 51, 52, and 53.

Bananas Flambé

GOURMET INTERNATIONAL ™

1/3 cup butter or margarine
3 tablespoons brown sugar
1/4 cup light corn syrup
3 tablespoons lemon or orange juice
1/4 teaspoon grated lemon or orange rind
4 bananas, cut in half crosswise and lengthwise
1/4 to 1/3 cup Cointreau, brandy, or rum, optional
Whipped cream, optional

Melt butter or margarine in blazer pan of chafing dish over direct high flame. Stir in next 4 ingredients. Heat, stirring constantly. Add bananas; spoon syrup over fruit; turn banana pieces carefully until glazed, about 5 minutes. Place pan in water jacket to keep hot for serving. If desired, before serving ladle warmed Cointreau, brandy, or rum over fruit; ignite. Serve when flame dies. Serve plain or topped with whipped cream. Yield: 6 to 8 servings.

APRICOT, PEACH, OR PEAR FLAMBÉ: Follow recipe for Bananas Flambé above and substitute 1 can (1 pound 14 ounce) apricot, peach, or pear halves, drained, for bananas. Serve plain or topped with whipped cream or toasted slivered almonds. Yield: 4 to 6 servings.

Caribbean Flambé

Follow recipe for Bananas Flambé above; add 1/2 cup washed, seedless green grapes to bananas as soon as glazed. Cover and heat. Flame if desired. Yield: 6 to 8 servings.

Cherries Jubilee

1/3 cup sugar
2 tablespoons cornstarch
1/8 teaspoon salt
1 cup cherry syrup (drained from canned cherries)
1 1/2 cups drained canned pitted Bing or sweet cherries
2 teaspoons lemon juice
1/4 teaspoon grated lemon peel
1/4 teaspoon almond extract
1/3 cup brandy or kirsch, optional
1/3 cup toasted slivered almonds, optional

Mix sugar, cornstarch, salt, and cherry syrup together in blazer pan of chafing dish. Place over direct high flame and cook until sauce is clear and slightly thickened, stirring constantly. Stir in cherries, lemon juice, lemon peel, extract, and 2 tablespoons brandy or kirsch, if used; heat. Place pan in water jacket to keep hot for serving. If desired, before serving pour remaining brandy or kirsch over sauce and ignite. When flame dies down spoon onto vanilla ice cream or cake à la mode. Sprinkle with toasted slivered almonds, if desired. Yield: 6 servings.

PEACHY-PECAN DUMPLINGS (PAGE 57)

Peachy-Pecan Dumplings GOURMET INTERNATIONAL™

See photo at left.

2 packages (12 ounce) frozen sliced peaches,
  defrosted
1 cup prepared biscuit mix
1/2 cup sugar
1/3 cup chopped pecans
1/3 cup milk
2 tablespoons melted butter or margarine
1/2 teaspoon cinnamon
Whipped cream, optional

Pour peaches into blazer pan of chafing dish or heavy fry pan on table top butane unit over direct high flame. Cover; heat fruit steaming hot. Combine biscuit mix, 1/4 cup sugar, pecans, milk, and butter or margarine; stir until dry ingredients are moistened. Drop heaping teaspoonfuls of dough onto hot fruit. Mix remaining sugar and cinnamon; sprinkle over dumplings. Cover; steam until dumplings are cooked and fluffy, 10 to 15 minutes. Serve plain or top with whipped cream. Yield: 6 servings.

Variations

Follow recipe for Peachy-Pecan Dumplings (above); change as suggested below.

PEACHY-RASPBERRY DUMPLINGS: Substitute 1 package (10 ounce) frozen raspberries for 1 package of peaches. Yield: 6 servings.

RASPBERRY-PECAN DUMPLINGS: Substitute 2 packages (10 ounce) frozen raspberries for peaches. Omit cinnamon. Yield: 6 servings.

Fun-Do Sundae Sauce

Recipes galore can be found on pages 21-23. Prepare them in a fondue pot or blazer pan of chafing dish, as desired.

Mini Fried Fruit Pies

Are great "ice-breakers" for dessert-and-coffee parties. No fussing at party time and the guests fry their own. See recipe on page 18.

Custard

3 cups milk
1/2 cup sugar
1/4 teaspoon salt
4 eggs, beaten slightly
2 teaspoons vanilla
Nutmeg or mace, optional

Combine 2 cups milk, sugar, and salt in blazer pan of chafing dish over direct high flame, stirring frequently. Place in water jacket. Mix remaining milk, eggs and vanilla. Stir into hot mixture. Sprinkle spice over top, if desired. Cover; cook until set, 45 to 50 minutes. Yield: 6 to 8 servings.

Variations

Follow above recipe and change as suggested below:

CRÈME BRÛLÉE: Substitute half and half (half milk, half cream) for the milk. Omit spice. Chill in blazer pan. Just before serving, sprinkle top with 1/4 cup brown sugar; place blazer pan in pan of ice and broil 5 inches from heat source until sugar melts and bubbles, 3 to 5 minutes. Serve at once.

FLAMING CRÈME BRÛLÉE: Before serving spoon 3 to 4 tablespoons Cointreau or brandy over custard; ignite. Serve when flame dies down.

SOUPS AND CHOWDERS

No more satisfying way to start a meal for family or guests than with a tempting aromatic soup served handsomely from chafing dish.

Hot soup served in a gleaming chafing dish can set the stage for a fine dinner party, and served with hot crusty French bread it's just-right food to serve for lunch, a posh late-evening supper, or to the in-crowd after water-skiing or schussing over the slopes.

Try one of the easy-made soups that follow. All are quick, easy to do, great food!

Fish Chowder
See photo at left

1/4 cup butter or margarine
1/2 cup coarsely chopped onion
1 cup thinly sliced carrot
1 cup water
1 1/2 teaspoons salt
1/8 teaspoon white pepper
3 cups milk or 2 cups milk and 1 cup half and
    half (half milk, half cream)
2 tablespoons flour
1/2 teaspoon fines herbes blend
1 cup diced cooked peeled potato, optional
1 cup flaked cooked fish (tuna, salmon, or
    other fish)
1 tablespoon chopped parsley

Melt butter or margarine in blazer pan of chafing dish over direct high flame. Add onion and carrot and sauté until onion is tender. Add water, salt, and pepper. Cover; cook until vegetables are tender, 10 to 15 minutes. Combine 1/2 cup milk, flour, and fines herbes; stir in remaining milk. Add to vegetables; cook, stirring constantly, until slightly thickened. Add potato, if used, and fish; heat to serving temperature. Sprinkle with parsley. Yield: 6 to 8 servings.

Variations

Follow recipe for Fish Chowder and change as suggested below:

CLAM CHOWDER: Decrease butter or margarine to 2 tablespoons and sauté 2 slices bacon, diced, until crisp, in butter or margarine in blazer pan of chafing dish over direct high flame. Remove bacon bits; set aside. Omit flour and herbs. Substitute 1 pint clams and liquid for flaked cooked fish. Garnish with bacon bits. Yield: 6 to 8 servings.

BACON CORN CHOWDER: Omit butter or margarine. Fry 4 slices bacon, diced, until crisp, in blazer pan of chafing dish over direct high flame. Remove bacon from pan and save. Sauté vegetables in bacon drippings. Substitute 1/4 teaspoon leaf thyme for the fines herbes blend and 1 can (1 pound) cream-style corn for the flaked fish. Yield: 6 to 8 servings.

VEGETABLE CHOWDER: Add 1 package (10 ounce) frozen mixed vegetables with water. Omit flaked cooked fish. Yield: 6 to 8 servings.

SAUSAGE OR MEAT VEGETABLE CHOWDER: Substitute 1 pound fully cooked wieners or smoked sausage links, cut in quarters, or 1 can (12 ounce) luncheon meat, diced, for flaked cooked fish. Yield: 6 to 8 servings.

Oyster Stew

1 can (12 ounce) fresh or frozen oysters, defrosted
1 teaspoon salt
1 teaspoon celery salt
Dash of pepper
2 cups milk
2 cups half and half (half milk, half cream)
2 tablespoons butter or margarine
1/8 teaspoon paprika
1 teaspoon finely chopped parsley

Pour oysters and liquor into blazer pan of
chafing dish. Add salt, celery salt, and pepper.
Heat over direct high flame until edges of
oysters curl slightly. Reduce flame. Add milk,
half and half, and butter or margarine; heat to
serving temperature. Sprinkle with paprika and
parsley. Yield: 4 to 6 servings.

Creamy Potato Potage

2 tablespoons butter or magarine
1/3 cup finely chopped cucumber
3 tablespoons thinly sliced green onion
1 can (10 1/4 ounce) frozen condensed cream of
  potato soup, partially defrosted
1 soup can milk
1/4 cup sour cream
2 tablespoons chopped chives, optional

Melt butter or margarine in metal fondue pot
over moderate direct flame. Stir in cucumber
and green onion slices; cook, stirring constantly,
until vegetables are tender. Add soup and milk.
Cover; reduce flame and heat to serving temperature. Fold in sour cream. Ladle into soup
bowls; sprinkle with chopped chives, if desired.
Yield: 2 to 4 servings.

Canned and Frozen Soups

Favorite canned and frozen soups, for a few
or a crowd, may be heated as directed on can
label. Heat the number of cans of soup desired
with the liquids required in the blazer pan of
the chafing dish over direct high flame or on
stove, stirring often during heating. Transfer
blazer pan to water jacket, lower flame, and
keep warm for serving.

Mulligatawny

1/4 cup butter or margarine
1 cup (1/8-inch) thin carrot slices
1 cup thinly sliced celery
1 cup coarsely chopped onion
1 clove garlic, minced
1 cup chopped peeled apple
2 tablespoons flour
1 teaspoon salt
1 teaspoon curry powder
1/4 teaspoon nutmeg
Dash of pepper
2 cups water
2 chicken bouillon cubes
1 can (8 ounce) tomatoes, undrained
2 cups diced cooked chicken
1 cup milk

Melt butter or margarine in blazer pan of chafing dish over direct high flame. Add carrot,
celery, onion, and garlic to butter or margarine;
cook until vegetables are tender, stirring often.
Add apple; cook until tender. Stir in flour, salt,
curry powder, nutmeg, and pepper. Add water,
bouillon cubes, and tomatoes. Cook, stirring
constantly, until thickened. Add chicken and
milk; heat to serving temperature. Place blazer
pan over water jacket. Serve in bowls, plain or
over rice. Yield: 6 servings.

Fun-Do Soups

Quick made Fun-Do Soups (see recipe on page
25) may be prepared in chafing dish, if desired.

INDEX